Alain Badiou: Live Th

M000284052

Also available from Continuum:

Donna Haraway: Live Theory, Joseph Schneider
Fredric Jameson: Live Theory, Ian Buchanan
Gayatri Chakravorty Spivak: Live Theory, Mark Sanders
Hélène Cixous: Live Theory, Ian Blythe and Susan Sellers
Jacques Derrida: Live Theory, James K. A. Smith
Jean Baudrillard: Live Theory, Paul Hegarty
Judith Butler: Live Theory, Vicky Kirby
Julia Kristeva: Live Theory, John Lechte and Maria Margaroni
Slavoj Žižek: Live Theory, Rex Butler

Alain Badiou: Live Theory

Oliver Feltham

continuum

Continuum International Publishing Group
The Tower Building   80 Maiden Lane
11 York Road   Suite 704
London SE1 7NX   New York NY 10038

www.continuumbooks.com

British Library Cataloguing-in-Publication Data
A catalogue record for this book is available from the British Library.

ISBN-10: HB: 0–8264–9692–X
        PB: 0–8264–9693–8
ISBN-13: HB: 978–0–8264–9692–8
        PB: 978–0–8264–9693–5

Library of Congress Cataloging-in-Publication Data
A catalog record for this book is available from the Library of Congress.

Typeset by RefineCatch Limited, Bungay, Suffolk
Printed and bound in Great Britain by MPG Books Ltd, Bodmin, Cornwall

Contents

Acknowledgements   vi

Abbreviations   vii

1   The Althusserian Years: Epistemology and the Production
    of Change   1

2   Maoism and the Dialectic   32

3   Set-theory Ontology and the Modelling of Change   84

4   Live Badiou   136

Notes   140

Bibliography   152

Name Index   158

Acknowledgements

In the research and lead-up to writing this book in the summer and autumn of 2007 it was exchanges with other researchers that helped me find my way out of a dark valley – researchers whose own work is continually provoked by that of Badiou: Jason Barker, Bruno Besana, Ray Brassier, Lorenzo Chiesa, Justin Clemens, Elie During, Felix Ensslin, Zachery Lake Fraser, Sigi Jottkandt, Peter Hallward, Dominiek Hoens, Gernot Kamecke, Quentin Meillassoux, Nina Power, David Rabouin, Frank Ruda, Aaron Schuster, Tzuchien Tho and Alberto Toscano. I thank my colleagues and friends at the American University of Paris for their collegiality. Finally I salute my Italian and Australian families and thank them for their support while they passed through their own shadowy valleys in which sunlight was reduced to a thread – but a thread that can be followed, as only one knows how: Barbara Formis.

Abbreviations

The following abbreviations for Badiou's articles and books will be used
in the body of the text:

BE *Being and Event*
CM *Le concept de modèle*
CT *Court traité d'ontologie transitoire*
DI *De l'idéologie*
LM *Logiques des mondes*
MM 'Marque et Manque'
PP *Peut-on penser la politique?*
RM 'Le (Re)commencement de la dialectique matérialiste'
SI 'La subversion infinitesimale'
TC *Théorie de la contradiction*
TS *Théorie du sujet*
TW *Theoretical Writings*

Chapter 1

The Althusserian Years

Epistemology and the Production of Change

Introduction

「Le monde va changer de base」
'Le monde va changer de base'
'The Internationale', French version

It is early May 1968. Alain Badiou, a high-school philosophy teacher in Rouen, is scheduled to give the second part of a lecture in Louis Althusser's seminar on philosophy and science at the prestigious École Normale Supérieure.[1] Jacques Rancière, Etienne Balibar, Francois Regnault and Pierre Macherey are participating in the seminar which is attended by over three hundred people. The first part of Badiou's lecture, a stinging critique of positivist epistemology in cybernetics and structuralism and a careful dissection of Carnap on the mathematical concept of model, had already been delivered. His colleagues were awaiting not only a full demonstration of the concept of model but also an explanation of its import for the greater concerns of the seminar: the distinction between science and ideology, the question of the emergence of new knowledge. But Badiou's second lecture was postponed: the students hit the streets, the paving stones began to fly, and Badiou, already an experienced militant through protests against the Algerian War, joined the occupation of part of the École Normale. His chief role was to calm people down, including René Scherer, now the grand old man of philosophy at Paris VIII but then an affirmed anarchist, keen to rain typewriters down on the riot police who were battering down the front door.[2] When an apparent calm returned to the Latin Quarter and the École Normale carried on business as usual, Badiou's lecture was never rescheduled. However, a year later both lectures resurfaced in written form, published by François Maspero and prefaced by a warning that spoke of the text's 'theoreticism', assigning it to a 'past conjuncture' since now 'no longer can we name a target and not hit it'.[3] With this text, Badiou's early period comes to a close and his second, Maoist period begins. The text, just back in print, is *Le Concept de Modèle*.[4] Its target is the first object of the present chapter.

The following corpus of texts constitutes Badiou's 'early work':

- 'L'autonomie du processus historique', *Cahiers Marxistes-Léninistes* Paris: École Normale Supérieure, No. 12–13, juillet–octobre 1966, 77–89.
- 'Le (Re)commencement de la dialectique matérialiste', *Critique*, Tome XXIII, No. 240, mai 1967, 438–67.
- 'La subversion infinitesimale', *Cahiers pour l'analyse*, No. 9, June 1968 (Paris: le Graphe, 1968), 118–37.
- 'Marque et Manque', *Cahiers pour l'analyse*, No. 10, Jan 1969 (Paris: le Graphe, 1969), 150–73.
- *Le concept de modèle* (Paris: Maspero, 1970).

To complete this list one must add the exoteric texts: a series of documentaries in which Badiou interviewed the leading French philosophers of the day – Raymond Aron, Georges Canguilheim, Michel Foucault, Jean Hyppolite, Paul Ricoeur – on philosophy's relation to sociology, science, psychology and language. Then one must add the less exoteric interview with Michel Serres, subtitled 'Concept of Model, the film'.[5] Finally, the most important exclusion from this philosophical corpus is that of Badiou's earliest work which is literary. In 1964, at the tender age of 25, Badiou published his first novel, *Almagestes: Trajectoire Inverse*, one of a trilogy including *Portulans*, published three years later, and a third novel, *Bestiaires*, that never appeared – giving rise to the tempting hypothesis that his entire philosophical project is a substitute for the completion of an impossible literary trilogy.[6]

The present text is itself an impossible substitute: billed as a short introduction to Badiou, it introduces the reader to his oeuvre by following his own introduction of his name into the field of philosophy. It begins at the beginning and attempts to *briefly* – first impossibility – restitute the initial context of Badiou's work: Althusser's distinction of historical materialism and dialectical materialism, and of science and ideology; and Jacques-Alain Miller's critique of Frege's foundation of arithmetic. A long introduction would restore the place of Sartre and Bachelard in Badiou's philosophical ancestry, and reconstruct his complex relation to the dominant intellectual movement of the time, structuralism, not to mention his all too brief naming of respectable adversaries in the persons of Quine and Carnap. But of course – and this is the second impossibility – there is no such thing as a 'long introduction'; there are monographs, but a monograph is an entirely different animal. To introduce a philosophy is to open a door onto it as quickly as possible. If the reader doesn't simultaneously start reading *Being and Event*, or learning French to read Badiou's as yet untranslated works, then this introduction has not been quick enough.

But one cannot write an introduction to a philosopher's work – third impossibility – without interpreting that work. To periodize Badiou's oeuvre, to identify the projects specific to each period, to evaluate their fate, to map his separation from his masters, Althusser and Lacan, to posit the existence of an underlying problematic that unites the different periods: all of this is to interpret Badiou, to select and divide, choose and exclude particular philosophical themes. The interpretation I develop here proceeds via a comparative analysis of each period of his oeuvre: the early period of materialist epistemology, the Maoist period of the historical dialectic, the current period of philosophy and its conditions. The guiding thread for this analysis is the question of the relationship between the thought of multiplicity and the thought of change. However, in so far as this book is primarily an introduction to Badiou – fourth impossibility – it cannot satisfactorily fulfil the tasks of interpretation: this would require the systematization of my own concepts, concepts I begin to sketch in Chapters 2 and 3.

In this chapter, I identify Badiou's initial projects and explain how he disengages his own trajectory from the work of his master, Althusser. The second chapter reconstructs Badiou's Maoist period. The third chapter attempts to define a third period beginning with the text *Peut-on penser la politique*, centred on *Being and Event*, and continuing to the present day.

To return to the target of Badiou's first philosophical text, *Le concept de modèle*, its identification will depend on three lines of enquiry: first, Badiou's reconstruction of Althusser's conception of dialectical materialism as a theory of social change; second, his reworking of Althusser's science–ideology distinction; and third, his tentative use of the mathematical concept of model to think change in scientific knowledge. Each of these enquiries meets with a problem in Badiou's argument, diagnoses it, and identifies how Badiou modifies his trajectory in response.

Structural change in society

Althusser and the Marxist theory of social change

Within this limited corpus the most consequent text for identifying Badiou's philosophical starting point is his critical review of Louis Althusser's seminal works *For Marx* and *Reading Capital*. Badiou's article is entitled 'The (Re)commencement of Dialectical Materialism' and it appeared in the journal *Critique* in 1967. To situate this text one must start by presenting the elements of Althusser's project that prove to be the most important in Badiou's eyes.

Althusser himself – and this goes a little way towards explaining the formalism of Badiou's reconstruction of his project – works at one remove from the classic Marxist concepts of the capitalist mode of production and the fundamental contradiction between the relations of production (the worker–boss relationship) and the forces of production (the resources, labour-power and technology at hand). For Althusser these terms belong to the science of society that Marx inaugurates in *Capital*, the science called 'historical materialism'. This discipline is quite distinct from the philosophy initiated by Marx's discoveries, the philosophy called 'dialectical materialism'. Dialectical materialism is concerned with developing a general theory of practice (economic, social, scientific), of global or structural change in practice, and with the distinction between science and ideology within the field of theoretical practice. Althusser understood this distinction between historical materialism and dialectical materialism and his own theoretical innovations as interventions designed to clarify the confused situation of Marxism. Ever since Khrushchev's speech at the Twentieth Congress denouncing Stalin, the gulags and the cult of personality there had been, in his eyes, a poisonous flowering of liberal–humanist interpretations of Marx. Coupled with this revisionism there was a refusal on the part of the French Communist Party – of which Althusser was a member – to discuss theoretical questions and question what Althusser delicately refers to as the 'practical problems' of Marxist politics. These were the main motivations underlying the theoretical and pedagogical initiative recorded in *For Marx* and *Reading Capital*.[7]

In his review of these texts Badiou identifies an unfinished task in Althusser's philosophy; the theorization of structural change in society and in the domain of scientific knowledge. In 'On the Materialist Dialectic', a key text for Badiou's exegesis, Althusser begins this task by attempting to identify the specificity of the Marxist theory of historical change, otherwise known as the dialectic. His working hypothesis is that Marxism lacks an explicit theoretical formulation of the dialectic; in other words, Marx never wrote a book on dialectics as a method, but that this method is already implicitly at work in both *Capital* and in key Marxist political texts.[8] Among the latter he chooses certain letters in which Lenin tries to explain how a proletarian revolution, contrary to Marx's predictions, occurred in a backwards country that had not even witnessed the triumph of the bourgeoisie and capitalism.[9] According to the *Communist Manifesto*, it is only when the contradiction between the relations of production and the forces of production is exacerbated to the point of incompatibility that a revolution becomes possible, a proletarian revolution which collectivizes the ownership of the means of production. In contrast, on the basis of Marx's concept of unequal development, Lenin argued that what actually played a crucial role in creating the instable situation of 1917 was not one but a whole series of contradictions each of which reinforced the next, making Russia into what Lenin famously called the 'weak link' of the chain of imperialist great powers. Althusser seizes this argument as clear evidence of the difference between a Marxist dialectic and the Hegelian dialectic. Hegel was Marx's master – as Althusser was Badiou's – and in the absence of an explicit formulation of the Marxist dialectic the default model of change – in Althusser's eyes – is always Hegelian; and as such it leads to theoretical and political problems. In the Hegelian model of change, a unity splits into opposing moments or forces thus forming a contradiction. Over time, this contradictory antagonism creates a new unity that negates the earlier separation, a unity that conserves some of the qualities of the earlier stages and yet contains something new. Our concern here, of course, is not fidelity to the complexity of Hegel's dialectic, but how Badiou's trajectory is affected by Althusser's characterization of Hegel.

Countering the thesis of a simple unity at the origin of change, Althusser argues that for a Marxist historical change begins within an always already given complex structured totality. Subsequently, the beginning of historical change does not contain in any manner the figure of its end, in contrast to the teleology of the Hegelian model which promises a return to unity, a final synthesis. Note that for Althusser Hegelian teleology is no straw target but an internal threat in that it underwrites the well-established interpretation of Marx known as 'economism', a tendency Engels himself fights during the Second International. Economism claims that capitalism develops in a univocal and teleological manner: the contradictions of the economy will inexorably lead, by means of whatever historical accidents and detours, to a proletarian revolution and socialism. The last aspect of the Hegelian model of change concerns the location of the motor of the dialectic, the very agent of change: it is present everywhere and yet nowhere.[10] In contrast, Althusser stipulates that in a strictly Marxist model of change the motor of change must be a particular element of the complex totality – and so in the case of social change, a particular social practice. When Marxists speak of Hegel's 'idealism' they are referring precisely to the impossibility of locating the agent of change.

But the Hegelian model is not the only rival to emerge in the thinking of change: one can also construct a *transcendent* model of change in which the agent or motor of change exists independently of and separate to that which changes, whether the latter be society, or a field of knowledge. Just such a model is at stake in Aristotle's analysis in Book 7 of the *Metaphysics* of a builder's production of a new house. Althusser identifies a further rival – the *mechanist* model of change – in which change also occurs as the result of something external, but this time it is a multiplicity of forces that are not unified into a single agent endowed with intention; the consequent change is arbitrary. In contrast, Althusser prescribes an *immanent* model: one in which the motor of change resides within that which undergoes change.

When Badiou reconstructs Althusser's theory the location of an immanent concrete agent of change forms a major concern: he calls it the problem of *structural causality* (RM, 449). Another major concern for Badiou is to account for the consistency of the social whole: this is what is lacking, in his eyes, from Althusser's theory of social change; there is no concept of the totality of social practices.

But why must one account for the consistency of the totality when the goal is precisely to think its transformation and thus dissolution? It so happens that in order to think change, one must be able to identify two different points or states of affairs between which change occurs; these might be the starting point and the endpoint of the change – but not necessarily since the change might continue indefinitely before and after these two points. If one cannot identify two separate states of affairs between which the change occurs, one is forced to oscillate between two incompatible theses: either everything is continually changing, or everything is absolutely the same. Either every single parameter in a given space is in continual variation and so measurement is impossible or all parameters are completely static. To think a specific change one must be able to identify what is changing and how it changes. In Althusser's case what is at stake in his reading of Lenin is theorizing the passage – via revolution – from capitalist society to socialist society and so he needs to be able to identify not only the consistent structure of capitalist society, and the consistent structure of the society that emerges through the change, but he must also think the change itself *as a consistent process* rather than a haphazard multidirectional affair. He does so by positing that social change happens within a structure that has a number of invariants. The first invariant is that any society is structured both by a dominant contradiction and by secondary contradictions.[11] The second invariant is that the dominant contradiction is determined and conditioned by each of the secondary contradictions: this conditioning is what Althusser, after Freud, calls 'overdetermination'. These secondary contradictions may exist within the domains of religion, ideology, the judiciary, international relations and the political system. The third invariant is that the dominant contradiction is always economic and so in capitalist societies it is the contradiction between capital and labour. This is how Althusser formulates Marxist principle of the 'determination in the last instance' by the economy.[12] According to Althusser's reading of Lenin's analyses and also Mao's classic essay *On Contradiction*, what happens in a revolutionary change is that these secondary contradictions 'condense' or 'accumulate' their determinations of the dominant contradiction to form a 'unity of rupture'.[13]

Althusser's argument caused a furore in Marxist circles: their main objection, as he characterized it, was that if one substitutes a pluralism of determinations for the monism of the Marxist conception of history, one destabilizes or calls into question the fundamental law of the development of capitalism, the law that guarantees the passage to socialism. For Althusser, such an argument fell into the category of economism and its rigid teleology: he returned to Marx's 1857 Introduction to the *Grundrisse* to show that what economism failed to take into account was the unequal development of contradictions within different societies. Nevertheless, at one level at least, Althusser's critics were quite right: the account of overdetermination and the plurality of contradictions does result in the simple recognition that the passage from capitalist to a socialist society is not a historical necessity. There is no longer a teleology to history: if historical change does occur, it does not slowly but surely realize a predetermined end or an internal necessity. It is precisely at this point that modality enters the theory of social change: the key modalities of change being impossibility, possibility, necessity and contingency. Much later on in his work, after he and Badiou parted ways, Althusser confirmed the anti-teleological import of his theory of change by explicitly embracing *contingency*, re-baptizing his philosophy an 'aleatory materialism' or a 'philosophy of the encounter'.[14]

Badiou's theorization of consistency

For Althusser the social whole consists of a set of interlocking practices: in his commentary, Badiou criticizes Althusser for positing this combination and hierarchy of practices without having first theorized the actual space in which these practices are placed (RM, 458). It is here that Badiou first turns to mathematics for aid in resolving a philosophical problem. If there is any 'mathematical turn' in Badiou's work with *Being and Event* it is in truth a *return*; his philosophical work starts in partnership with mathematics, specifically with regard to the task of theorizing the collective unity – the consistency – of Althusser's 'always already given complex structure'. This mathematical theory must meet two other requirements: first, this structure of practices must be endowed with a hierarchical order; second, one must be able to account for the overall change of this order. In response to the first requirement, Badiou assumes that to posit an order it is sufficient to determine a maximum, or a 'dominant practice'. Note that in *Logiques des mondes*, published forty years later, to construct an order one must first demonstrate the existence of an orientated relation between any two given elements and then the existence of a minimum element. Back in 1967 the dominant practice is given the role of both unifying and dictating the identity of its particular structure: for instance, the dominant practice in a given social structure might be juridical, ideological, or religious, and so this practice will give that society its particular historical identity.

In response to the second requirement Badiou declares that change can be understood as the displacement of the dominant practice (RM, 456). The question is then what causes such a displacement. Althusser develops an immanent model of change and so the cause of change must be a locatable part of society: Badiou calls it the 'determining practice'. In line with the fundamental theses of Marx's historical materialism, the determining practice is always the economic practice (RM, 457). The subsequent difficulty for Badiou's reconstruction and theory of structure is that this practice must both form part of the interlocking hierarchy of *determined* practices and at the same time be present at another level as the *determining* practice. The starting point of change is thus in a position of *internal exclusion*; that is, it is internal in that it belongs to the order of determined practices, but at the same time it is excluded from that order since it determines the latter. This is the question of 'structural causality': note that the extent of Badiou's flirtation with structuralism in this epoch consists in finding echoes of the question of structural causality in Levi-Strauss's concept of the zero-signifier, an echo which loses its importance in proportion to the multiplication of other echoes, such as with Spinoza's concept of *natura naturans* (SI, 128; RM, 457 n. 23).

Badiou fulfils these requirements for a theory of structure by constructing a mathematical structure that can be read as a 'conjuncture'; that is, as a unified order of social practices including both a dominant and a determining practice. There are two salient features of this mathematical construction for our enquiry. First, rather than directly working on a set of elementary practices, Badiou uses the mathematical concept of function to order a set of 'instances' where each instance is an articulation of two practices: a practice placing another practice (RM, 461; LC, 64). This proto-ontological construction is thus not atomistic but relational at base. Second, Badiou's construction both orders these instances and includes an instance that determines which instance is dominant; this relationship of determination is held to model the form of change. However, the weak point of this construction is that the initiation and intensity of change, and any possible variation in its form, cannot be theorized. Change is evident, says Badiou, which may be true from a macroscopic perspective on history, but certainly not at the level at which a militant philosophy is supposed to intervene; the level of a particular political practice (RM, 455). In Chapter 2 I will have reason to baptize this macroscopic perspective on change since it is a voice that resurfaces again and again in Badiou's philosophy. In this mathematical structure the one window which Badiou does leave open is the direction and effect of this change; its modality is pure possibility in that it is completely open which of many practices will become the dominant one if change occurs.

But there are further problems with this theory of change: Badiou argues that economism – a target he adopts from Althusser – consists in the identification of the dominant practice with the determining practice, the practice that changes a conjuncture. Thus according to economism all societies are dominated by economic practice (RM, 457). Yet it is not clear how Badiou's position – all societies are determined by economic practice, where determination consists in the selection of the dominant practice – avoids economism in turn. Moreover, in this mathematical structure the order of practices is quite unified, but at the price of eradicating any possibility of the emergence of a new practice: change is theorized as the reshuffling of the same practices into a different order. According to my diagnosis, what lies behind these problems is the influence of a figure whose shadow extends far further than that of Hegel: Aristotle.

Change or genesis: the return of Aristotle

For a seasoned reader of Badiou there is one peculiarity about his reconstruction of the problem of structural change, and that is his uncritical repetition of Althusser's use of the term social 'totality' or 'whole'. Throughout the rest of his oeuvre his critique of totality is constant; and even in this very text he singles out in passing Sartre's use of totality as ideological (RM, 451 n. 18). This peculiar silence is compounded by Badiou's assertion that the dominant practice is responsible for *both* the hierarchy of practices within the totality – their order, their degrees of relative autonomy – *and* for the overall unity of the totality (RM, 456, 461). Moreover, as mentioned above the determining practice – the practice responsible for historical change – selects the practice that will newly take up the dominant position, thus reorganizing both the hierarchy and the overall identity of the social totality and producing a new conjuncture. When Badiou speaks of the historical change of the conjuncture, he says that the effect of change in the conjuncture is confused with the effect of its very existence. Badiou thus identifies a fusion in Althusser's theory between the principle of change, the principle of order and the principle of the unity or existence of the social whole.[15] In other words, for Althusser the process that causes social structure to change is the same process that determines the existence and internal order of society. At one point in his text, Badiou does recognize that these three questions – of change, order and existence – can be thought separately. He argues, quite correctly, that Althusser simply assumes the existence of the structure of places, whereas in fact neither the account of determination (change) nor the account of domination (order) can generate the 'collectivizing concept of the instances', that is, the unified existence of the whole.[16]

What is at stake in Althusser's fusion of these three questions is the creation of a model of change in which any transformation of the whole is thought in the same terms as the genesis of the whole. In other words, there is only one type of change and it is at work in both the formation and in any global transformation of a society. This vision is a result of what can be called the *productivist model of change*, according to which the being of change is thought under the paradigm of the technical production of goods. In Aristotle's *Metaphysics* the development of this model is explicit: being is thought as substance, substance is thought under the category of cause, and a causal analysis is developed through the analysis of the artificial production of new substances such as houses or tables. Aristotle distinguishes four causes of production: the efficient cause or agent of change; the material cause or raw material that undergoes change; the formal cause or pre-existing design; and the final cause, the goal of the process, a finished product. Althusser explicitly reproduces this Aristotelian and productivist schema when he theorizes the general structure of practice: he speaks of the raw material, the means of transformation – which include both the design and the agent – and the finished product.[17]

The effect of this underlying Aristotelian schema in Althusser's work is the fusion of the questions of change, order and existence. In the productivist model of change, change occurs to something – a substance for Aristotle, a society for Althusser – in the form of the genesis of that something. The account of change is thus an explanation of how a substance or society acquires unity and order. In Aristotle's analysis of production, a substance acquires unity in the shape of a union of its form and its matter, and acquires an order according to which form dominates matter.[18]

The productivist model of change results, as we saw, in the problems of economism and change being thought purely as the reshuffling of existing elements. It can be countered in three points. First, one can argue that it is not necessary to posit the existence of unitary agents that govern and guarantee the existence and order of change. Second, one can contest the idea that change is predominantly finite, that it has simple start and endpoints: change can be thought of as continual but with varying rates and intensities.[19] Third, within the example of artificial production itself, one can argue that the product is not a finished unity but rather enters into a web of interactions within its practical context of use that continually affect its identity.[20] As we shall see, Badiou takes up these ideas in his later thought of change but under different headings, notably in his focus on infinite multiplicity, and specifically in his insistence in *Being and Event* on the incompletion of change and the collectivization of agency.[21]

Aristotle himself provides one key for surpassing the productivist model of change and its focus on genesis. When he distinguishes natural productions – genesis and destruction – from artificial productions, he argues that in the latter the material cause pre-exists and outlasts the actual process of change. To avoid the fusion of change with genesis, the matter that undergoes change must exist in excess of that change. That is, something has to *remain the same* during a change, otherwise one cannot speak of a change occurring *to* something. What remains the same is the *hypokeimenon* or substrate, the underlying matrix that bears all the properties of a particular substance. Twenty years after his critical reconstruction of Althusser, Badiou adopts a similar solution; he thinks change as an infinite process of supplementation of an already existent structure, and in doing so he makes use of a concept quite close to the *hypokeimenon*, the generic multiple, which as a whole bears no one property yet parts of it bear every property. However, the generic multiple is not what remains the same but precisely what brings about change in being brought to presentation.

In *Théorie du sujet*, the final work of Badiou's Maoist period, Badiou advances his own diagnosis of the model of change he inherits from Althusser in his early work. The main limitation of what he renames the 'structuralist dialectic' is that it presents a deterministic and over-complete theory of change: as we noted no room is built in for contingency or variations in the process of change, but more importantly change itself is limited to modification rather than full-scale transformation.

However, the theory of social structure was not the only foothold that Althusser's work afforded Badiou for an examination of the thinking of change. Much of Althusser's early work was devoted to theorizing transformations in the field of scientific knowledge, specifically that of Marx's development of historical materialism. It is in this context that Badiou develops his own articulation of science and ideology in reaction to Jacques Alain Miller's alliance of the two in the famous article 'Suture'.

Structural change in knowledge: science and ideology

Epistemological break as infinite process

The entire distribution of tasks within Althusser's project can be derived from his primary claim: an epistemological break occurs between Marx's early philosophical work, focused on Feuerbach's problematic of man, and his scientific work, inaugurated in *Capital*.[22] As a result of this break not only did the entire field of investigation change but the scientific concepts Marx developed through the study of classic political economy no longer allowed him to even reconstruct the Hegelian and Feuerbachian categories of man or consciousness. For Althusser, this cut generates not just one but two disciplines: first, the new science itself, historical materialism, whose object is the history of the production of societies; second, dialectical materialism, a new type of philosophy whose object is the history of theoretical production.[23]

Althusser claims that he simply borrowed the concept of epistemological break from Bachelard. Etienne Balibar has shown how he in fact
subjected the concept to considerable revision.[24] For Bachelard an epistemological break designates the slow gradual process through which a
science disengages itself and its results from the common knowledge of
its time, which is a tissue of error and illusion. For Althusser, on the
other hand, science disengages itself from ideology, but the latter is not
simply the epistemological negative of science. Ideology possesses a social
function: that of determining how individuals experience their economic and political living conditions. For Althusser, an epistemological
break is both an event – he dates it quite precisely in the case of Marx –
and an infinite process. As such, at no moment can one pronounce the
break complete and designate a discourse as pure science without any
inmixture of ideology. Inasmuch as ideology plays a social role it is an
irreducible part of scientific discourse. The conflictual relation between
science and ideology is thus a permanent fixture for Althusser. Consequently science must perform a constant work of purification in order
to extract its results and its own proper objects from the *doxa* of the
times. Moreover, this is not a secondary task for science but its primary
task; the very core of scientific work for Althusser consists in this continual separation from ideology. In the general domain of theoretical
production, the very objects that a science initially takes as its matter
for investigation are constituted by an ideology.[25] Just as in Bachelard's
conception, for Althusser science gradually distinguishes its own
objects from the objects given in common, ideologically filtered, experience. Moreover it is only inasmuch as this distinction between kinds of
objects has taken place – and the epistemological break is occurring –
that a discourse can actually be identified as an ideology. That is,
it is solely from the perspective of a science – Althusser's example
being Marx's historical materialism – that an ideology can be diagnosed
as such – classical political economy as an instance of bourgeois
ideology.

Althusser claims that the primary function of philosophy as dialectical materialism is to develop a theory of the history of theoretical
production: at a local level this means tracing a line of demarcation
between science and ideology in the field of theory. The practical task
of philosophy is thus to divide science from ideology. This conception
has two consequences whose repercussions echo throughout Badiou's
oeuvre. The first is that philosophy arrogates the task of reflexivity from
science: it is not science itself that examines its own theoretical production but philosophy. As a result science is not auto-intelligible but blind
and thus machinic in its production of new knowledge. This conception

of science is not specific to Althusser, it is a classic philosophical conception found, for example, in Husserl's *Crisis of the European Sciences*.[26] The second major consequence of Althusser's conception of philosophy is that philosophy doubles the movement of science itself in its endless division of its own concepts and new objects of knowledge from the ideological context in which their elements are found. Philosophy must thus engage in an infinite process of division within the field of knowledge; this prescription remains part of Badiou's own conception of philosophy to this very day. The third consequence of philosophy's ceaseless division of the field of theoretical production into science and ideology is that it becomes difficult to position philosophy itself. Indeed in the debate on the nature of philosophy that took place between Althusser and his students (Rancière, Macherey, Balibar, Badiou, etc.) between 1965 and 1968 it is this very problem that formed one of Badiou's bones of contention.[27] The difficulty of placing philosophy with regard to other practices will remain one of Badiou's chief concerns.

It is in relation to this Althusserian context that Badiou begins to develop his own position with regard to science and ideology, specifically by targeting an author close to him in both generation and institution: Jacques-Alain Miller. Miller was one of the founding members of the *Cercle d'Épistémologie* group at the École Normale Supérieure, responsible for publishing the short-lived but influential journal *Cahiers pour l'Analyse* between 1966 and 1969. Miller published his 'Suture: elements for a Logic of the Signifier' in the first issue and Badiou published his reply, 'Marque et Manque: à propos du zéro', three years later in the last issue.[28]

In his article, Miller develops a close if unorthodox reading of Frege's construction of the whole number series in *The Foundations of Arithmetic*.[29] Frege defines a number as an attribute of a concept: he states, 'The number which belongs to the concept F is the extension of the concept "equinumerical to the concept F"'.[30] The 'extension of a concept' is the number of objects which fall under a concept, that is, those objects of which the concept is true. For Frege, a number such as four cannot be attributed to one concept alone, but to all concepts that subsume the same number of objects; that is, a number is always assigned to a set of concepts. For this reason the 'extension of a concept' occurs on two different levels of the definition: the first as 'the extension of the concept *equinumerical to the concept F*'; and the second as part of this very concept *equinumerical to the concept F*. Frege defines the equinumericity of concept F with concept G as the existence of a one-to-one correspondence between the objects that fall under each of the concepts.[31] In the case of the definition, the objects that fall under the concept *equinumerical to the concept F* are actually other concepts, all of which have equal numericity – or the same extension – as the concept F. To understand Miller's interpretation of Frege what one needs to retain is that the construction of a number depends on objects being subsumed under concepts.[32] In order to construct the number zero Frege thus requires a concept whose extension is zero; that is, a concept under which no object falls: he chooses the concept of a non-self-identical object. Frege assumes there are no such objects based on his commitment to Leibniz's principle of identity, according to which the truth of judgements depends on the identity of their objects. His subsequent task is to define the operation of succession which will bind together the whole number series by defining its order. The first instance of this operation of succession is naturally the passage from the number zero to the number one. Frege establishes this passage by defining the concept 'identical to zero' under which one object alone falls: the number zero. The number one is thus the extension of the concept 'identical to zero'. When Frege defines the general operation of succession between any two cardinal numbers, n and m, he employs the concept 'belonging to the natural series of numbers ending in n'. The extension of this concept is the number m, which happens to be the successor of n on the condition that the natural series of numbers begins with zero.[33] For instance, the number of objects (numbers) that fall under the concept 'belonging to the natural series of numbers ending in 3' is only four if one counts zero, and four is the successor of three. Hence in the Fregean construction of the series of whole numbers, the operation of succession counts zero for one each time.

In his reading of Frege Miller poses the following question: 'what is it that is operating in the series of whole numbers, what does their progression base itself on?' His answer: 'in the process of the constitution of the series, in the genesis of the progression, the function of the subject – misrecognized – operates'.[34] Miller bases this claim on a strong isomorphism between Frege's non-self-identical object and the subject of the signifier as defined by Lacan. Like the subject, the non-self-identical object is lacking from the symbolic order – in Frege's case, the order of concepts that subsume objects.[35] Moreover, like the subject, this nonexistent object is nevertheless counted at the level of the concept – it generates the zero – and within the operation of succession it is also counted-for-one.[36] For this reason Miller terms the zero 'the place-holder of a lack' which is precisely the role that Lacan assigns to the unary trait or master signifier in identifying the subject within the field of the unconscious. This combination of operations – the summoning and subsequent exclusion of the non-self-identical object, its substitutive institution as zero and its repeated counting-for-one in the generation of the series of whole numbers – is precisely what Miller calls *suture*.

At first sight all we have here is a particularly striking analogy, but Miller, as mentioned above, claims that the subject is at work in the genesis of the whole number series. Moreover, in the prolegomena to his argument proper he declares:

> What I aim to reconstruct, bringing together teachings scattered in Lacan's oeuvre, should be designated under the name throughout: logic of the signifier – a general logic in that its operation is formal with regard to all the fields of knowledge, including that of psychoanalysis; that is in specifying itself within the latter, it rules it . . . The logic of the signifier . . . does not follow the laws of logician's logic . . . prescribing their jurisdiction, it falls outside their jurisdiction.[37]

Thus by means of the isomorphism between the subject and the Other, and the zero and the whole number series Miller expands what he calls the logic of the signifier from both linguistics and the psychoanalytic clinic to cover all fields of knowledge. Subsequently in scientific discourse there must always be a substitute, a placeholder for the lacking subject.

Badiou's epistemology of logic

Evidently Badiou cannot admit this argument because in enveloping all theoretical production within a generalized logic of the signifier it renders impossible the science ideology distinction. His goal in 'Marque et Manque' is thus to save this distinction and in his opening remarks he situates Miller's text in the following terms:

> For us both Frege's ideological representation of his own enterprise and the rerun of this representation in the vocabulary of the Signifier, lack and the place-of-the-lack, mask the pure productive essence, the process of positions whereby logic, as machine, never lacks anything apart from what it produces elsewhere. The logic of the Signifier is a metaphysics. Representation of representation, intra-ideological critical process-progress.

To make good this claim Badiou develops an Althusserian epistemology of logic as a machinic production of stratified writings. However, twenty years later in his book-length study of mathematical attempts to define number, *Number and numbers*, Badiou returns to Miller's non-mathematical text, admitting that he has not yet finished with its arguments. He writes 'I am there, I am still there' using precisely the same phrase that he uses a decade later to describe his Maoist commitments.[38] In his latter critique he marshals Russell's paradox as the obstacle to Frege's definition of sets as the extension of a concept and suggests that if the logic of the signifier is indeed equivalent rather than merely analogous to Frege's construction, then any logical inconsistency affecting the latter will also affect the former.[39] This suggestion is not followed up but the persistence of the critique of Miller is enough to indicate that what is at stake is an indirect and incomplete gesture of distancing with regard to structuralism. In *Théorie du sujet*, structuralism is critiqued in the form of Althusser's structural dialectic, but not in terms of its basic commitment to a differential articulation of signifiers. The final index of Badiou's inability to have done with Miller takes precisely the form of a wandering signifier: *suture* is the very term Badiou uses in *Being and Event* to name the relation between a situation and the void of its being.

In 1969, however, Badiou's concern was to critically delimit Miller's enveloping of logic by developing his own epistemology of logic. In doing so he uses an Althusserian template: first, in line with Althusser's analysis of theory as a practice with its own raw material and means of production, he analyses logic not as an ideal language or a paradigm of rationality but as a differentiated mechanism of production whose product is regulated and stratified writings. Second, in line with Althusser's definition of the task of philosophy, he sets out to detect and remove the layers of ideology to be found in logicians' own representations of their scientific activity. In the case in hand he dismisses Frege's recourse to concepts, the subsumption of objects under concepts and self-contradictory objects as ideological and metaphysical. He shows that mathematical logic has no need of such notions by demonstrating how zero can be constructed in an alternative manner within mathematical logic by using logical notations of predicates, reflexivity and relationships between variables. Furthermore, following Bachelard, he shows that the role of the principle of identity in science does not concern objects, but rather an inaugural confidence in the identity of marks (those of formal writing) and of science's technical and experimental apparatus.[40] For this reason science does not so much lack the non-self-identical thing – Miller's subject of the unconscious – but forecloses it; science has no relation to such an entity.

In his analysis of logic as a practice Badiou divides it into three mechanisms which produce and divide types of writing: the mechanism of concatenation which determines the stock of marks to be used and the basic syntax; the mechanism of formation which forms sequences of such marks and then divides them into well-formed formulas and ill-formed; and the mechanism of derivation which in turn divides the well-formed formulas into the derivable and the non-derivable. He uses these distinctions to show in his construction of zero that one never finds in logic, as Miller argues, a mark of lack, but rather one finds lacking marks. For example, Badiou's notation for zero $0(x)$ – which reads 'x is a zero in so far as x is not identical to itself' – is a well-formed formula and so it exists at the level of the mechanism of formation. However, this formula for zero is rejected by the mechanism of derivation and so this particular mark can be said to 'lack' at the level of derivation. Badiou concludes that marks lack in logic only inasmuch as they are restituted on another strata of its inscriptions. Moreover these marks at no point subsume some non-self-identical object.

Badiou draws two conclusions from his argument. The first is that science does not suture the subject and does not fall into the domain of ideology: the multiplicity of its stratified orders is irreducible to any one order of the signifier – note the early emergence of a concept of inconsistent multiplicity. The second conclusion is that it is philosophy itself, as a particular region of ideological practice, which sutures science under ideological categories such as 'man' and 'truth', thus effacing science's epistemological break. To understand Badiou's conception of science and its implications for his greater project first one must consider what he does with the science–ideology distinction once it has been saved from psychoanalysis.

In Badiou's reconstruction of Althusser's argument, the distinction between science and ideology takes place within a dialectical process in which their coupling is irreducible. Hence the distinction *cannot operate as a norm* because neither of the terms is given as primary: the science–ideology couple is inaugural. Moreover the distinction is non-distributive; one cannot simply divide the field of practices by distributing each of them into one of the two categories (RM, 450).[41] Finally, as mentioned above, the distinction can only be made retroactively; that is, it is only from the position of a particular science that one can identify and delimit a particular ideology. There is no universal definition of ideology allowing its immediate recognition and disqualification. Following Althusser, Badiou holds that the irreducibility of the science–ideology couple is also marked by the spontaneous emergence of ideology within scientific work: in 'Marque et Manque' he gives the example of Frege's epistemology of logic and much later in *Being and Event* he signals the positivist philosophy accompanying the mathematical innovation of certain set-theorists (MM, 156).[42]

Retroactive identification and spontaneous emergence do explain how science and ideology form a couple, but not how they form a dialectical process. To do so Badiou must introduce philosophy: philosophy recuperates and appropriates the products of science by interpreting its operations in the terms of classical philosophical categories. In particular Badiou picks out the categories of totality, truth, sense and the subject as ideological: truth for instance, when applied to logic, is a term that conceals a multiplicity of different mechanisms of selection (MM, 150,155; CM, 38/98).[43] From a Marxist standpoint, the subject, contrary to Lacan's speculations on the subject of science, is also an ideological category (MM, 158; RM, 449 n. 16). Note that in his later work Badiou rehabilitates both truth and the subject for what will remain for him the proper task of philosophy: thinking the invariants of change – only the notion of totality will be permanently rejected. Science, in turn, reacts to philosophy's inaccurate representations of its operations, and develops new concepts. It is this pattern of appropriation and reaction that generates a dialectic between science and ideology, with philosophy playing both the role of ideology and a go-between. However this still does not explain why this dialectic is a process and why this appropriation and reaction are repeated. To understand the dynamic at work we need to turn to Badiou's understanding of science.

Science and the machinic production of novelty

In the last pages of 'Marque et Manque' Badiou expands his epistemology of logic into a conception of science itself as a self-sufficient, impersonal, machinic and stratified multiplicity. Science is self-sufficient inasmuch as it has no need of other ideological or social practices in order to produce its marks; it is impersonal inasmuch as it has no relation to the subject, constitutive or concealed; it is machinic in so far as it is continually productive of sequences of marks and finally it is stratified in that these marks are divided by mechanisms that place them on different strata. But not only does science continually produce new sequences of marks, it also produces new strata of writings. In his study of logic Badiou spends most of his time distinguishing and establishing the three mechanisms of concatenation, formation and derivation and their concomitant strata. However, he also mentions a fourth strata which is obtained by turning the predicate of zero – rejected by the mechanism of derivation – into a constant and adding it to the derived formulae (MM, 160). In his article 'Subversion infinitésimale' Badiou examines this kind of operation at length, describing it as a mathematical performative, a baptism that opens up a new domain of writings by converting one modality into another. That is, a mark that is *impossible* in one strata – such as the square root of minus one – is given a name – *i* for an imaginary number – thus opening up another *possible* series of numbers. Such operations of naming thus generate new strata of writings: Badiou terms this proliferation of strata 'machinic' since at this point of his work there is no subject at stake in the emergence of novelty.

At the high point of his argument Badiou swiftly claims in a few lines and a brief footnote that science as a productive machinic multiplicity forms the realization of Derrida's project in *Of Grammatology* and *Dissemination*, and Foucault's project in *The Order of Things*. He declares that if one wishes to 'exhibit writing as such, and absent its author, if one wishes to obey Mallarmé's injunction that the written Work take place without subject or Subject, a radical secular means exists to the exclusion of any other: entrance into the writings of science whose law is such' (MM, 162 n. 18).[44] In the last pages of *The Order of Things*, Foucault announces the birth of a new epochal regime of knowledge, an 'episteme'; one that was heralded in the writings of Nietzsche and whose major sign will be the erasure of the category of man. Badiou claims that science, 'the scriptural Outside without blindspot' – perhaps a recycling of Blanchot's term – is a movement within which 'one will never encounter the odious figure of man'.[45] If ever Badiou situates himself with regard to what came to be known in the English-speaking world as 'post-structuralism' it is in these pages at the very outset of his career. Whether or not such a conception of science could realize Derrida and Foucault's tasks and projects is an open question; though one should note, as mentioned above, that it depends upon a classic philosophical conception of science. Forty years later, in his preface to the new edition of *Concept de modèle* Badiou is amazed at how mathematical logic formed the very destination for thought in his first book of philosophy.[46]

There are two further aspects of Badiou's early conception of science to be put in place before it can be evaluated with regard to the project of thinking structural change in the field of theoretical practice. The first, a thesis inherited from Bachelard and Althusser, is that science as a practice is marked by the production of new objects of knowledge: it produces novelty (RM, 450).[47] The second principle, also an element of the Bachelardian and Althusserian lineage, states that the knowledge produced by science is objective. Etienne Balibar explains that rather than critically questioning science's pretension to objectivity and then installing a fictive guarantee of its knowledge – such as the transcendental subject – or worrying about the incompatibility of science's objectivity with its history, Bachelard's initial gesture is to posit the objectivity of scientific knowledge. Bachelard is then able to show that this inaugural thesis alone allows one to think the history of science not as the mechanical result of a series of external influences but as the history of the production of concepts.[48] The place of this principle in Badiou's work shifts. Its negative correlate remains more or less stable in that Badiou maintains his distance from any Kantian epistemological investigation of the legitimacy of knowledge claims.[49] If one were to locate its positive formulation – 'scientific knowledge is objective' – in his reconstruction of Althusser, it would probably be in his acceptance of the declaration that historical materialism is a science. However, the definition, concepts and tasks of this science are not present in any of Badiou's early texts, so the Bachelardian–Althusserian gesture must be located elsewhere. In his 1992 article on Althusser, Badiou reveals that his master always chided him for his 'Pythagorism', his over-reliance on mathematics, and claims that like many strong-willed disciples, he reacted by simply exaggerating the supposed fault.[50] Indeed Badiou's eventual split with Althusser is not just political, it is philosophical and its stakes include the status of mathematics. The place of the Bachelardian –Althusserian gesture is thus Badiou's declaration that mathematics is ontology. Consequently, if one compares Badiou with Althusser it is indeed mathematics that takes the place of the famous 'science of society', even in his early work; hence philosophy maintains the position and tasks of 'dialectical materialism'. Many of the complaints addressed to Badiou's set-theory ontology – *It's too abstract! How does it theorize capitalism? What about social relations?* – thus betray a desire for just such a total science of society.[51]

In the absence of a total science of society, what use can Badiou make of his conception of science in the project of thinking consistent structural change?

At first sight it appears that science as a proliferating multiplicity of strata offers a spectacle of unending, continual and unpredictable change. Science is continually remaking itself and expanding its strata.[52] But how useful is this for Badiou's purposes? To think the transformation of imperialist bourgeois society into a classless society, Badiou needs to theorize a global change between two different structures. If therefore he has established the existence of multiple and continual change, what he then needs to do is insert some distinct states or identifiable zones into that flux and this is precisely what he does in an appendix to his article on Gödel's theorems. The object of the appendix is to trace the successive philosophical recuperations of Gödel's mathematical results in idealist epistemologies. The function of this short history is to *periodize* machinic change into a dialectical alternation between mathematical construction and its ideological recuperation (MM, 172).[53] The dialectic of science and ideology mentioned above has thus found its dynamic and the source of its repetition but at the price of giving philosophy an inordinate role in constructing such a dialectic. In his Maoist period, under the dictate of the primacy of political practice, Badiou will search again for a solution to the problem of the periodization of dialectical change: it forms the central preoccupation of his *Théorie du sujet*.

If Badiou contributed nothing else to philosophy, this materialist epistemology of logic, this careful untangling of ideological categories and mathematical constructions would have secured him a place in the university libraries. Apart from the Marxist terminology, he could be quite simply arguing for more accurate philosophy of science. It's clear that in Badiou's eyes there is room for a non-Fregean philosophy of mathematics, one that takes into account the scientific work of Frege, Carnap, Russell and Quine without making the same philosophical choices as they do with regard to the import and range of this work.[54] This is precisely the line of investigation he follows in *Le Concept de modèle*, dividing logical positivism's contributions to the theory of models and semantics from its importation of this theory into a general epistemology of formal and empirical sciences (CM, 22–8/69–80). However, this line of enquiry was cut short before it bore enough fruit to establish its credentials: cut short by politics. It is my thesis that this cut not only periodizes Badiou's work but that the division occurs within *Concept de Modèle*. It is this internal break that forms our destination in the next section.

The mathematical concept of model and scientific change

Models and their powers of differentiation

We have come full circle. In his first lecture on 29 April 1968 in the packed Salle Dussane, Badiou set out to critique an empiricist use of the

category of model in both its vulgar version – found in Levi-Strauss and
Von Neumann's remarks on method – and in its sophisticated version –
Carnap's work on the syntax of scientific language. In the vulgar version, a theory is said to be an abstract model of a particular region of
reality, and the model is adjusted so that it resembles reality. In the
sophisticated version, a model is correctly understood as an interpretation of a formal system; that is, one starts out with a formal system
of axioms and theorems and then one defines a semantic field of variables that are made to correspond to the formulae of the system via a
series of rules. The logical positivists claimed that within a scientific
domain, the formal system could be found in the structure of its deduc-
tions whereas the semantic fields could be found in the 'observation
statements' concerning scientific objects. They defined rules of correspondence that linked the syntax of a scientific discourse to its semantic interpretation in terms of scientific objects. Note that this presents an
inversion of the vulgar empiricist use of the term model: it is not the
formal theory which is the model but rather its semantic interpretation
in terms of a set of scientific objects; that is, a particular field of scien-
tifically measured phenomena is said to model the theory. Badiou does
not critique logical positivism for its use of the concept of model; he
simply explains it and then formulates a mild objection; this modern
intra-logical apparatus is thus used to restitute an older philosophical
and empiricist dichotomy between formal science and experimental
science.

Badiou's own project is to develop what he calls a 'progressive' epistemological use of the concept of model, which is no small ambition.
To this end, Badiou pedagogically reconstructs of the concept of model.
He shows how once the formal syntax has been constructed, the semantic field chosen and its variables assigned, one must then show that the
axioms of the formal syntax still prove to be consistent within the chosen
semantic field. In Badiou's terms, the result is 'a structure is a model of a
formal theory if all the axioms of that theory are valid for that structure'
(CM, 44/107). I invite the reader to explore the details of this
reconstruction of the concept of model in the text itself; for our purposes what matters are the epistemological principles Badiou identifies
in the course of his argument.

The first of these principles is immanence: the construction of the
concept of model depends entirely on the mathematical theory of
sets, which it does not set out to demonstrate. To build a model one
has recourse to the mathematics of whole numbers and the axiom of
induction. To speak of a model is thus to presuppose the 'truth' or

existence of these mathematical practices (CM, 42/104). Thus, contrary to logical positivism, the use of models does not relate formal thought to an 'outside' such as empirical phenomena, nor are scientific statements verified through procedures of observation and measurement. A model is unfolded within a domain of interpretation that is immanent to mathematics (CM, 52/123). Badiou then takes this point as the occasion to lay out a fundamental epistemological principle, one that could form a blazon for a school and one that distances him again from Frege's project: 'One establishes oneself within science from the outset. One does not reconstitute it starting from nothing. *One does not found it*' (CM, 42/104, my italics). Consequently if there is an experimental and verificational dimension to mathematical practice, it does not occur in the form of the artificial production and measurement of phenomena, but rather in its actual writing, in the consistent articulation of its marks: in particular, in the semantic placing-into-correspondence of a formal syntax (CM, 34,53). Contra Frege the principle of identity in science for Badiou, following Bachelard, concerns the identity of scientific instruments and experimental apparatus, not the purported identity of objects. In the case of mathematics, formulae must consist of material marks subject to laws of invariance: an x must always stand for an indeterminate variable submitted to each of the constraints declared in a particular formula.

The second epistemological principle to emerge in Badiou's argument concerns differentiation and change within mathematics and it is far more difficult to grasp. Before formulating this principle we need to examine Badiou's three different accounts of models and what he terms their 'powers of differentiation'. The first concerns the difference between logic and mathematics. Very early in the text he raises a classic Althusserian question: 'What is the *motor* of Science (in the sense that class struggle is the motor of history)?' (CM, 19/63). It is Althusser's Aristotelian conception of practice, mentioned above, which allows Badiou to apply an apparently political question to scientific practice. Thirty pages later he answers – countering the supposed transhistorical status of logic as the essence of Reason – that it is the gap *between* the implicit use of logic during demonstrative practice *and* its explicit formalization as a specific historical apparatus (intuitionist logic, classical logic, para-consistent logics, etc.) that is the motor of the history of logic (CM, 47/113). The second account of the differentiating effects of models concerns the difference between mathematical and logical structures. Badiou shows how it is only when mathematical axioms form part of one's formal syntax that not all structures but only particular ones can form models of that syntax; his example is an axiom which cannot be satisfied by structures with only one element (CM, 49/115). On the other hand, when the formal syntax is made of logical axioms alone, any structure can serve as a model. One can proceed in an inverse direction: starting from a particular mathematical structure one can work out its syntactic form; again, Badiou's example involves universes that contain only one element, and he searches for their adequate axiomatic form. His conclusion is that '*a model is the mathematically constructible concept of the differentiating power of a logico-mathematical system*' (CM, 47–52/ 113–21).

Note that in the first two accounts of models what is important is the doubling of mathematical practice; certain parts of mathematics – the 'means of production' – are used to distinguish between different mathematical structures or logics. The difference between these two instances of mathematics does not seem to be a *motor* of change understood as a kind of agent; rather it appears to be a condition of possibility; mathematics can be used to produce new knowledge in mathematics. Such productive change thus remains immanent to mathematics rather than the mechanical result of an external force or of the application of an external discourse.

Badiou's third account of models and differentiation is far more complicated: it concerns the historical use of models by logicians and mathematicians such as Gödel to demonstrate both the coherency of different theories and the independence of particular postulates (CM, 62/140). For example in 1939 Gödel uses the construction of a model to prove that Zermelo–Fraenkel set theory remains consistent both when the Axiom of Choice is added and when the continuum hypothesis is admitted.[55] Badiou shows how the construction of a model of Euclidean geometry and, on its basis, a model of Riemann Plane Geometry, can be used to demonstrate the independence of the parallels postulate in Euclidean Geometry. That is, the postulate on which these two geometries differ – the postulate that through one point external to a line one and only one parallel line passes – is actually independent of the axioms that guarantee the consistency of Euclidean Geometry (CM, 64–6/ 142–5). In other words, the parallels postulate cannot be deduced from the other axioms.

Badiou then turns to examine the historical effect in mathematics of such proofs of relative consistency and independence. He admits that Gödel's proof of the consistency of Zermelo–Fraenkel set theory plus the Axiom of Choice – ZFC – came after the fact; most mathematicians had already chosen to use the axiom, thus *anticipating its certainty*. The effect of Gödel's proof is thus not to initiate but to *retrospectively transform* such a choice into an 'internal necessity' of mathematics (CM, 64/142). Again we have a conversion of modality: from the pragmatic *possibilities* opened up by using the axiom of choice to its *necessity* via the construction of a model.

In order to expand the concept of model into a 'progressive epistemology', Badiou seizes on precisely these temporal orientations of anticipation and the retroaction. Within the historical process of a science he proposes to call 'model', 'the status retrospectively assigned by a defined formal apparatus to the first practical instances via their experimental transformation' (CM, 67/148). The productive value of formalization lies in its double inscription of mathematics, mentioned above: that of using and reproducing certain knowledges – logic as a means of production – at the same time as constructing specific models to produce new knowledge – the differentiation of consistent theories. Badiou concludes:

> 'Model' designates the crossed network of retroactions and anticipations which weave the history of formalization: either what has been designated, with regard to anticipation, as a cut (*coupure*), or with regard to retroaction as a re-forging (*refonte*). (CM, 68/149)

These moments of anticipatory cut and retroactive reworking thus offer another conception of the periodization of the process of change in scientific knowledge. But this conception is not developed, Badiou does no more than sketch the general principles of his epistemology, and the conclusion to the text is abrupt. Indeed, it is not until *Being and Event* that one finds a sequel to this brief exploration of temporality of change: the future anterior – 'what will have been the case' – being the tense that organizes the enquiries constituting change on a local level; a tense that combines anticipation and retroaction.

Before addressing whether Badiou comes good on his promise to develop a progressive epistemology, one should investigate his other attempt to theorize the historicity of mathematical knowledge.

Transformational nominations in mathematics

In his essay 'Subversion Infinitésimale' Badiou provides another example of a careful application of the Althusserian conception of philosophy – the division of science and ideology within the field of science – but this time with regard to the existence of infinitesimals, presupposed in differential analysis and dismissed by Berkeley and Hegel. Again I shall leave the history of the infinitesimals to the curiosity of the reader; at the level of epistemological theses there are five clear stages to Badiou's argument. The first stage is his declaration that one of the peculiarities of mathematical writing is that unbound variables allow the place of an impossibility to be marked within a series of numbers: he calls these places 'infinity-points' (SI, 119). His key examples are: x where $x^2 + 1 = 0$, x thus being equivalent to the square root of minus one which is impossible within the series of real numbers; and y where 'for all x, $x < y$', y thus being an indeterminate infinite. The second stage consists in identifying historical moments in mathematics in which these impossible places are occupied by a new constant, when they are baptized and transformed into a new proper name. So, for example, the square root of minus one is named the imaginary number, I; and the first denumerable infinity is named the first aleph, $\aleph$, or ω. The third stage in Badiou's argument consists in indicating the new mathematical domains that have been opened by these transformational nominations; domains that remain mathematical in that all of the standard operations of the previous domain – multiplication, subtraction, addition, etc. – can be performed within them (SI, 120). Badiou terms this operation a 'transgressive extension', a term that finds its echoes twenty years later in *Being and Event*'s concept of the 'generic extension' of a situation. In the fourth stage Badiou introduces – for the first time in his work – an enigmatic Lacanian thesis whose role will do nothing but grow as his thought matures: *the impossible characterizes the real*. In this context, Badiou's gloss is that the impossibility of certain statements within a mathematical structure singularizes the latter by differentiating it from the new structure that renders those statements possible (SI, 122–3). A marked place of impossibility within a mathematical structure – such as the series of whole numbers or real numbers – thus harbours a power of differentiation and multiplication with regard to structures or series: it is this sense that it can be termed 'real'.[56] In the fifth and concluding stage of his argument Badiou states that the effect of these transformative nominations is a re-forging (*refonte*), that is a major reworking and reorganization of a science.

Throughout his oeuvre Badiou will maintain a concept of a transformative naming of the impossible – such as the intervention in *Being and Event* – to the point that it becomes what I name in the following chapter an entire voice or tendency in his thinking of change. The other henceforth permanent feature of Badiou's thinking is his citation of Galois' remark according to which he found his revolutionary ideas in the works of his predecessors, inscribed unbeknownst to them (SI, 128).[57] Badiou swiftly reinterprets this in a Lacanian framework as a return of the repressed: 'what is excluded from the symbolic reappears in the real: under certain conditions what is specifically excluded from a mathematical structure reappears as the inaugurating mark of the real (historical) process of the production of a different structure' (SI, 128). In his reconstruction of Althusser's problematic of structural change Badiou argues that the initial point of change has to be in a position of internal exclusion, a practice present in the structure but not represented. In this article he adds an epistemological criterion: the initial site of change is an idea that is presented but not yet known or recognized as such. This is very close to Lacan's punning definition of the unconscious as *l'insuccès* (failure) or *l'insu-qui-sait* (the unknown which knows). Badiou then claims that 'in science just as in politics it is the unnoticed (*l'inaperçu*) which puts revolution on the day's agenda' (SI, 128). But is this general point, which is no more than a faint analogy, enough to link his epistemology to progressive politics?

How can an epistemology be progressive?

Both of these texts – which carefully disentangle mathematical practice from previous philosophical and ideological interpretations – end with the concept of re-forging (*refonte*) and with incomplete gestures towards its importance for thinking political change.[58] The context of these gestures is the provision of a solution on the part of *Concept de Modèle* and 'Subversion Infinitésimale' to the Althusserian problematic of thinking consistent change in a complex structure. Mathematics furnishes us with a conception of the production of new knowledge via both the experimental construction of models and the occurrence of transformational nominations. The problem, however, with these solutions is that they answer the demands of what Althusser called 'dialectical materialism' and its concern to theorize theoretical production. They do not answer the demands of historical materialism, the science of society, which is consecrated to thinking social and political change.

The limitations of Badiou's solution in *Concept de modèle* are revealed in the penultimate chapter by the paucity of his assertions concerning the existence of an indirect relation between the field of his work – the 'theory of the history of the sciences' – and proletarian ideology. He cites Althusser's doctrine that philosophical practice carries out the class struggle in the domain of ideology and claims that 'this intervention' – his text – is characterized by 'its reflected relation to *one* particular science: historical materialism; and conjointly, its relation to proletarian ideology' (CM, 62/138). Inasmuch as this reflected relation is nowhere elaborated upon in the text, save in this passage, this is an incomplete gesture whose impatience is only exacerbated when he closes by restating Althusser's doctrine on philosophy – 'In the last instance, the line of philosophical demarcation has as its practical refer- ent the class struggle in ideology' – and adds the gloss that 'the stakes of this struggle are the class-appropriation of scientific practice' (CM, 62/ 138). Admittedly this is the terminology of another political con- juncture, one whose stakes one can only fail to understand through hasty judgements made from today's perspective – if, that is, we possess any- thing so consistent as a perspective nowadays! But note that the question of the relationship between science and politics is here opened up and then immediately closed under the overarching political concept of class. What is most striking about this passage is that these remarks remain gestures; when one examines Badiou's conclusion as a whole it is evident that he does not export his results into the domain of historical materialism, into the domain of political and social change; he restricts his argument to the question of the historicity of mathematical formalization.

The 'warning' that prefaces the original edition of *Concept de modèle* diagnoses the text of *theoreticism* and states 'the time for missing one's target is over' (CM, 7/40). The editorial collective were thus evidently referring to the absence of an exportation of epistemology into politics. There is some evidence, however, that this absence is no mere accident. Badiou spends the first part of the text criticizing the logical positivists for their illegitimate exportation of the concept of model into an empiricist epistemology. In the 1968 televised interview with Michel Serres, called 'Modèle et structure', both Serres and Badiou develop a joint condemnation of literary structuralism for its inaccurate and over- expansive exportation of a concept of structure from linguistics. But this is misleading; it is not a matter of banning *any* exportation of concepts from one discipline to another – Badiou has never been purit- anical about institutional boundaries. Indeed to his amusement Serres develops an accurate use and analysis of literary *structure* in Molière's play *Don Juan*. Hence certain exportations are sanctioned. The question with regard to Badiou's early period is whether or not an exportation from dialectical materialism to historical materialism – from the produc- tion of new knowledge to the production of new social relations – can actually be theorized. Moreover this is not only a question for Badiou's early work since in *Being and Event*, all change, whether political, artistic, scientific or amorous, will be thought of in terms of the construction of new knowledge.

Despite such instances of continuity in his philosophical oeuvre, it is in the period immediately subsequent to the publication of *Le concept de modèle*, the Maoist period, that the most drastic rupture takes place: Badiou drops all epistemological investigations of mathematics. When he does employ mathematics it is in the philosophical work that closes this period, *Théorie du sujet*, and moreover it is in a strictly analogical fashion. His argument is thus vulnerable to precisely the kind of attack on illegitimate and inaccurate exportation that he himself wields against the logical positivists and structuralism. Subsequently he removes this vulnerability, but at the price of rehabilitating ontology in *Being and Event*. Once one declares that all discourses make ontological claims in terms of unity and multiplicity, that mathematics is the most rigorous discourse on the existence of unity and multiplicity and that mathematics itself is ontology, then there can be no 'exportation' of mathematics since its structures are said to schematize the existence of any situation whatsoever. But as we shall see in Chapter 3, the rehabilitation of ontology creates other vulnerabilities, inviting the twin accusations of a metaphorical use of mathematics and the development of an unanchored, unverifiable and irredeemably abstract ontology.

There is an answer to these accusations, and it is very simple. In the last pages of this book it will take us back, full circle again, to the concept of model.

Theoreticism and the primacy of practice

Where does this leave us in our investigation of Badiou's early philosophical work? Precisely with its punctuation by the 'warning' prefacing *Le concept de modèle*. The collective presiding over the *Théorie* series published by Maspero baldly state that its theoretical conjuncture has passed, that the time has come in which one can no longer aim at a target and miss it, that its domain is 'limited' and 'very indirect', and that 'the struggle, even ideological, demands an entirely different style of work and a lucid and just political fighting spirit'.[59] This judgement is based on an assertion of the primacy of political practice – since the *Theses on Feuerbach* one of the axioms of Marxist philosophy – and it will go on to dominate Badiou's Maoist period. What is not yet clear to this collective, nor to Badiou, is that in the absence of an analogical exportation of the concept of model, in his patient pedagogical elaboration of its details, and in his exhortations to the reader to complete the exercises,

Badiou had already granted a primacy of practice: to mathematics, not politics. But this orientation was to be set aside for twenty years in response to the call of the events of May. In December 1968, after the restoration of de Gaulle's government, and after the sad procession of intellectuals quitting the stormy waters of revolution to moor in the silt-bound harbour of parliamentary democracy, for Badiou it was time to change approach; it was the time of politics.

Chapter 2

Maoism and the Dialectic

Introduction: there is no science of history

> 'Science of history? *Marxism is the discourse that the proletariat as subject bases itself upon* – this must never be forgotten.'
>
> *Théorie du sujet*, 62

In the 1970s texts, no other sentence signposts Badiou's Maoist turn as clearly as this one, and no other sentence seeks to bury his Althusserian past quite so decisively. It declares that there is no historical materialism, no 'science of history' whose theoretical framework – for Althusser – was then to be made explicit by dialectical materialism. In its place Badiou declares that Marxism is the systematization of the militant experience of class struggle. The very orientation and nature of Marxist discourse is thus affected by what, for the Maoists, is its first axiom: the primacy of practice. Evidently this is the great Maoist contribution to guarding against the academic absorption of Marxism as one among many curious political theories to be archived. The problem, however, is that it is no longer clear what place is reserved in this activist Marxism for the grand concepts of mode of production, or commodity fetishism, etc. What consistency remains in a discourse that is suspended from an aggregate of particular political struggles; how can it still be given a single name? Closer to home, how can we reconcile Badiou's development of three theories in this period – a theory of ideology, a theory of contradiction and a theory of the subject – with the doctrine of the primacy of political practice? Badiou himself appears to reconcile the two with a softer formulation of the doctrine in his *Théorie de la Contradiction*: 'Marxism is primarily a taking of a political stand and a systematization of partisan experience; secondarily it is a science of society.'[1] Yet this minimal hierarchy still does not clarify the relationship between the two orientations of Marxism.

This chapter concentrates on three of the longer, more theoretical texts from this period of Badiou's work: *Théorie de la contradiction* (TC), *De l'idéologie* (DI) and especially *Théorie du sujet* (TS).[2] To date each of these works remains untranslated and so in the English-speaking world, apart from the exploratory trips of a few individuals, these waters remain largely uncharted.[3] I shall demonstrate in this chapter not only why *Théorie du sujet* should be in every high-street bookstore but more importantly how it joins *Le concept de modèle* as a text on the cusp of a new period, a turning text, a sustained investigation that explores and expands Badiou's Maoism to the point of transforming it into something else, for which in the early 1980s there was not yet a name. In other words, *Théorie du sujet* completes Badiou's Maoist period. Yet it closes its own period with a gesture of incompletion, the gesture that is the chief sign of the following period, the period of *Being and Event*.

At its outset Badiou's Maoism begins with a simple thesis: there is truth in a political revolt.

The Maoist turn: the primacy of practice

Truth in revolt

In Badiou's previous project – developing a materialist epistemology of mathematics – truth, along with the subject, was condemned as an ideological category, one that cloaked a diversity of mechanisms of selection and stratification. In his mid–1970s essays *Théorie de la Contradiction* and *De l'idéologie*, we witness a rehabilitation of the category of truth, though it will turn out, in the end, to be a matter of selection and division again (TC, 13). In *De l'idéologie*, the context is a polemic on the subject of ideology directed against Althusser's 'Ideology and Ideological State Apparatuses' and Deleuze and Guattari's *Anti-Oedipus* (DI, 20–8,38–40). Badiou's main argument is simple: there is more than one ideology. That is to say, any theory of ideology must account not only for the dominant ideology but also for the possibility of a 'proletarian ideology', otherwise one cannot explain the occurrence of revolt. Against Deleuze and Guattari Badiou insists that even if the masses are not duped into believing in the dominant ideology but desire and subjectively identify with it, one still needs to explain Spartacus and the slave revolt. He sarcastically demands whether the slaves rebelled while identifying with the Romans' representation of them as animated tools. The starting point of any analysis of ideology for Badiou is rather a social conflict, such as a strike in a factory, and the subsequent emergence under pressure of divergent ideologies (DI, 28–30). In other words, the analysis of ideology should focus on a local instance of the class struggle, keeping in mind – and this is Badiou's other maxim – that both the exploiters and the exploited are perfectly conscious of their interests and the existence of exploitation; contrary to those theorists who conceive ideology as the duping of the working class, as 'false consciousness'. For Badiou there is always a spontaneous knowledge on both sides of the class struggle of its stakes (DI, 4).

Within a situation of conflict the ideological space divides according to how social relations – employer–worker relations – are represented: as amenable to conciliation or as essentially antagonistic, as contingent and changeable or as necessary and permanent. In turn these divergent representations can be analysed not as images or illusions but rather as the material expression of class interests; the content of a trade unionist's argument is real in that it ultimately represents the social and financial interests of the bourgeoisie. Badiou reminds his readers that this is a basic materialist thesis: thought is driven by external material forces, and in a strike it is those forces – physical, financial – that are brought to bear through discourse. It is thus in this context that the term *force* first makes its appearance, a key term in the 'historical dialectic' that Badiou develops in *Théorie de la contradiction* and *Théorie du sujet*. In an ideological conflict over working conditions or pay what these forces drive is a process of division whose continuation depends on whether or not the resistance and the conflict develop into a revolt. It is within such revolt – and this is a thesis that Badiou guards to the present day – that a new thinking is generated (of justice, social organization and politics) and that elements of a proletarian ideology emerge (DI, 34–6, 45). The problem is, however, that these elements remain as dispersed as the knowledge the exploited develop of their own oppression; geographically and chronologically scattered in different struggles (DI, 92). This proletarian ideology suffers from its contingent and multiple birth: it risks evaporating into inconsistency just as Badiou's own discourse risks what Marxism calls 'spontaneism'; excessive trust in particular revolts without any heed paid to strategic questions of organization. What is required is a dose of *consistency* and in this period of Badiou's oeuvre the medicine is readymade: the Marxist dialectic of history and the party.

There is truth in history

The Marxist dialectic enters Badiou's text in the form of an existential thesis: there is a long-term historical project of the exploited classes beneath and beyond any particular struggle. Note that change is rendered consistent by positing a *hypokeimenon* – the historical project of the proletariat – as the unifying support of dispersed political events. This project is rendered necessary by the objective and irreducible antagonism between the working class and the bourgeoisie (TC, 9–10). In *Théorie de la Contradiction*, in his commentary on Mao's maxim 'it is right to rebel against the reactionaries', Badiou states emphatically that 'the essence of the proletarian position holds in its historical project, not in particular revolts' (TC, 9). Moreover in this text – which we should remember is as much a political pamphlet as a theoretical text – Badiou returns to a teleological vision of history, speaking of the 'ineluctable foundering' of the world of oppression and exploitation. There are two names for the *universal agent* of this process of transformation, for the subject of history: the 'revolutionary masses', and the 'proletarian class' (DI, 51, 57, 71). It is in the gap between these two names that Badiou's Maoism is played out. On the side of the masses and their rebellion Badiou posits that whatever the historical conjuncture, whether it be Thomas Munzer and the peasants or the Taiping revolt, there are a number of 'communist invariants' present in the insurrection, namely a claim of equality, a critique of private property and a critique of the state (DI, 58–61). This hypothesis of 'communist invariants' sows some consistency among the dispersed revolts. However, from the standpoint of class, of the proletariat, Badiou claims that these communist invariants are insufficient, and only in so far as they are taken up and directed by Marxist-Leninist theory can they contribute to the formation of a revolutionary proletariat and a possible overturning of property relations (DI, 87).

It is the extension and expansion of isolated revolts into sustained revolutionary action that takes place according to the dialectic; which is to say, according to a historical process of division driven by contradictions between opposing social forces. For Badiou not only does a truth emerge in revolt, but there is also a truth of the entire dialectical process. As the astute reader will have recognized at this moment Badiou's thought is unashamedly Hegelian; in fact he cites Lenin's own approval of the passage in the *Science of Logic* on the absolute idea being the identity of the practical and the theoretical idea (TC, 3, 6).[4] The question remains, however, just how the practical idea – the communist invariants – will be unified with the theoretical idea – Marxist-Leninism – during the political process.

Both of Badiou's Maoist manuals are in large part consecrated to this question. In *Théorie de la contradiction* Badiou states 'The thought of the exploited who revolt is always to be articulated and unified with the dialectic, which is the thought of that thought' (TC, 14). Note the resemblance with Plato's definition of philosophy as the thought of thought. This statement is produced at the end of a long commentary on Mao's principle 'it is right to rebel against the reactionaries' in which Badiou claims that a revolt can be reinforced by the consciousness of its own rationality; that is, through Marxist theory developing the revolt's knowledge and returning it – no doubt in pamphlet form (TC, 11).[5] This theoretical development of the knowledge of the revolt consists, according to Mao, in the systematization and concentration of the ideas of the masses (DI, 88).

The instrument of that systematization is none other than the revolutionary Party, as conceived by Lenin. The party is Badiou's *third* name for the subject of history inasmuch as its role is the directive articulation and organization of class struggle according to the communist project (DI, 6; TC, 8, 12, 45). It is at this point that Badiou rehabilitates the category of the subject; contrary to Althusser, it is not the mere effect of ideology but the party itself *as* the material organization of revolutionary action. In Badiou's oeuvre the name of such a subject will change, but henceforth this conception of the subject as the organization and effectuation of global change at a local level will remain, as will the basic description of its work: *division*, the subject exists as a division. In Badiou's Maoist period, the subject-party systematizes the masses' ideas by dividing them according to a class analysis; certain ideas are revisionary and ultimately serve bourgeois interests, other ideas are revolutionary (DI, 72–3). In doing so the party participates in what Badiou calls the 'dialectical cycle of revolutionary knowledge' which is another term for the historical formation of a proletarian ideology (DI, 69–72, 113). In the introduction to this chapter I stated that Badiou's challenge was to reconcile the primacy of practice with his construction of theories of ideology, contradiction and the subject. For a Maoist, of course, any reconciliation of an opposition must occur practically, over time, in a dialectical process. And indeed for Badiou it is within the actual development of revolutionary knowledge that theory emerges from its dialectic with political practice. This process consists of five stages: first, various ideas emerge in a dispersed manner during a mass revolt: Badiou terms this an 'ideal force'. Second this force splits due to class

struggle within the revolt during which the ideas are partially system-
atized into old and new ideas. Third, a party practising a Marxist-
Leninist class analysis systematically places these divided ideas. Fourth,
the party translates these ideas into directives for action. Finally the
realization of these directives both produces new dispersed ideas and
evaluations of their correctness and so the cycle begins again as ideal
force. Far from being impractical and esoteric Marxist theory resembles
commonsense: if one idea doesn't work, try another.

What does not resemble commonsense is the idea that a party could
evaluate the correctness of directives for action; surely that is the role of
opinion polls and public relations agents! If we examine closely Badiou's
conception of the party it turns out not to be definitively anchored to
the Leninist conception of centralized hierarchical organization. Badiou
says that the emergence of the revolutionary directing class within a
revolt is signalled by the emergence of revolutionary knowledge (DI,
81). The proletariat's ability to organize itself into a party is no more
than its ability to systematize the masses' correct ideas. The existence of
an organization is completely dependent on the existence of a certain
type of knowledge. In terms of our periodization of Badiou's oeuvre,
what we have here is a continuity: the knowledge-society isomorphism
inherited from Althusser's 'dialectical materialism'. Badiou's concerns
are thus still epistemological. But this is not the only blurring of our neat
periodization. In *De l'idéologie* he cements the knowledge-society isomorphism in what he calls his *essential* thesis: 'the proletariat is a logical
force' or 'the proletarian organization is *the body of a new logic*' (DI, 100,
98, my italics). This is precisely the task that he sets his category theory
logics, thirty years later, in the last book of *Logiques des mondes*: theorizing
the emergence of a new collective body – a new consistency – as the
material instantiation of change.

Badiou explicitly raises the question of the nature of the party
towards the end of *De l'idéologie*; he states that the question of whether or
not the organization of the proletariat takes the form of a centralized
party is one of the general struggles of thought. His position is that this
is not a subjective but a logical question. Objection! Logic is neither a
communist invariant nor part of the Marxist systematization of past
struggles. Nevertheless, Badiou defends its capacity to furnish solutions
by claiming that its machinic apparatus – in a return of the 'Subversion
infinitésimale' argument – shields it from the dominant ideology (DI,
98). Logic and mathematics thus neither completely disappear nor serve
as mere analogies in the second period of Badiou's work. The task
Badiou sets logic here is to develop a form of organization that will not

fold at the first defeat. The massive difference, however, between these early calls for a new organizational logic and the work in *Logiques des mondes* is that in the latter it is a not a matter of a pre-existing organization developing and rendering consistent ideas that emerge in a popular revolt, but of the *a posteriori* emergence of a new organization *consequent* to an event and *as* a movement of change. The late Badiou thus risks what the early Badiou rejects and dismisses as spontaneism: trust in the dispersed emergence of communist invariants.

Description and prescription: folding theory into practice

In 1976, however, Badiou's main concerns go under the names of the 'dialectical cycle of revolutionary knowledge', and the conditions for the emergence of a 'proletarian ideology'. If *Concept de modèle* was condemned for theoreticism, what kind of text is appropriate to these concerns? Its first quality – as many remark of Maoist texts – is that it must be pedagogical: even more pedagogical than *Concept de modèle* which sold over twenty thousand copies and was used in France as a introductory textbook to mathematical logic.[6] The pedagogical aspect signals that these texts are primarily political – they seek to inscribe themselves within if not direct and accelerate the very dialectic of knowledge they describe: as Badiou says at the beginning of *Théorie de la contradiction*, every Marxist text is both reflective and prescriptive, theoretical and directive (TC, 11). Two material features signal this extra-textual ambition; the first is that these texts – though figuring in the official Badiou bibliography under the subcategory 'political essays' – currently circulate in *PDF* form without Badiou's name. Instead of an author's name we have the name of the political party to which Badiou then belonged: The Union of the Marxist-Leninist Communists of France. Note that when *De l'idéologie* is attributed to Badiou, it is acknowledged as a collaborative work with François Balmès. The second feature is that these texts are called *fascicules*; partial manuals or guides that form part of a series. When one reads them one has the sense that a great deal of work remains to be done; Badiou himself promises at one point another fascicule on the role of intellectuals. The texts themselves are not incomplete but they do form part of an incomplete project.

That project, in its largest possible sense, could be nothing other than the proletarian revolution. But in the absence of the revolution in mid-1970s France, the question remains of the real practical context of these texts, especially given that the theory of dialectical cycle of revolutionary knowledge cannot start any historical process on its own (TC, 39).

That is to say, Badiou places all Marxist knowledge under the sign of Hegel's Owl of Minerva: the theoretical knowledge of historical change comes after practice, or, in a more tendentious formulation, Marx's *Capital* is the systematization of the proletariat's historical knowledge of revolt. In the terminology of *Théorie du sujet*, 'Scission as the site of forces posits the radical anteriority of practice over the intelligibility of the correlation' (TS, 53). Thus the very existence of these Maoist fascicules presupposes a prior practical context or 'correlation'. We are given a clue when Badiou describes the context of the theory of the dialectic in terms of the necessity of steering between a rightist deviation – revisionism (in philosophy, the metaphysics of identity) – and a leftist deviation – spontaneism (in philosophy, the theory of indeterminate flows). The primary practical context is thus the worker's political movement and ultimately the party itself as a site of division (TC, 30, 49). It is especially important to keep this in mind when faced with the apparently unanchored and indeterminate dialectic of *Théorie du sujet*.

The primacy of practice as the premise of a theory of historical change means that UCFML fascicules inscribe themselves within a context of political division: struggle is an absolute (TC, 18). In this period of his work Badiou holds that within the class struggle, destruction is a condition of the creation of the new. Thus, if anything is to come of these texts and their prescriptions, if an ideal force is to emerge, the texts themselves are doomed to obsolescence and destruction (TC, 13). Marxist theory, Badiou declares, is *always* a 'field in ruins' waiting to be remade. By consequence, it remains a field in ruins after these texts, after their period comes to an end.

Badiou's Maoist theory of the dialectic situates itself in a context of perpetual struggle and division, and projects its own obsolescence. Whether this is just another of philosophy's forms of self-overcoming or a genuine expulsion into strange waters remains to be seen. To understand Badiou's Maoist theory of the dialectic one has to come to terms with the only major work of this period: *Théorie du sujet*.

The structural dialectic and its periodization

The structural dialectic: *offsite* and *splace*

The first thesis advanced in *Théorie du sujet* is that an entire series of dialecticians are responsible for a limited and static concept of the dialectic. Althusser's dialectical materialism is the last expression of a line that passes from the Greek atomists directly to Hegel, then to Mallarmé and finally to Lacan. The first moment in Badiou's argument is thus a *synthesis*; the poet, the philosophers and the psychoanalyst are grouped together due to their contributions to what he calls the 'structural dialectic'.

If one steps back from the argument to consider method for a moment, one notices that it is at this point in Badiou's oeuvre that a distinctive style of philosophical interpretation emerges: each of these dialecticians thinks part of the structural dialectic in their own terms – the *clinamen* for the atomist, the vanishing shipwreck for Mallarmé – but the terms in which this dialectic is built – the *splace*, the *offsite*, *force* and *torsion* – are Badiou's own. The overall effect is that this theory appears to be held by each of these thinkers – due to the force of Badiou's inter-pretation – but at the same time, as the 'structural dialectic' this theory is not held by any of them in particular. What emerges from this synthesis is not Badiou's own position but a worthy adversary, one that comes close to reality, but not close enough (TS, 72–3).

The second step in Badiou's argument is to claim that the structural dialectic ineluctably fails to account for the actual movement of political history. It falls apart because it cannot think qualitative global change: it cannot think revolution. The third step is to announce the construction of an alternative theory, the *historical* dialectic, capable of thinking quali-tative change by means of a concept of the subject as the *torsion* of structure. To construct this alternative theory Badiou divides his authors – his masters – by means of concepts like 'force' and 'offsite'; separating out their contributions to the structural dialectic from their intuitions and anticipations of his historical dialectics. We could call this moment of division one of *analysis* though it does not resemble any analysis familiar to students of English-language philosophy; its goal being nei-ther the analysis of a philosophical text – such as Hegel's *Science of Logic* – nor the analysis of a particular phenomenon. The next move is to *extrapolate* these intuitions and anticipations into a theory of subjectivity as torsion. Again, this method may seem odd to a student of English-language philosophy: it is neither history of philosophy or pure phil-osophy; the interpretation of primary texts is mixed with building a theory. For readers of Deleuze this should prove no surprise. For the empiricists, however, this technique is suspicious: a theory of historical change should primarily be measured against concrete examples of historical change rather than other philosophies. But this is to suppose an anti-dialectical separation between theory and practice. Badiou's claim is that any Marxist text is itself the condensation of the militant political experience of past struggles. The theory of the historical dialectic is itself an *expression* of a particular historical conjuncture. In *Théorie du sujet* the trace of that conjuncture – marked by May 1968 in France and the Cultural Revolution in China – is the insistence that a dialectical theory account for global political change. The result is not an entirely different dialectic but a supplement to the structural dialectic: Badiou keeps the same basic terms and then literally adds a few twists.

First the basic terms: all structure consists of elements – called *offsites*, or *outplaces* (*horlieu*) – and a space, a whole, to which the elements belong and in which they are placed – the *splace* (*esplace*).[7] In his early reconstruction of Althusser Badiou speaks of practices and their relative place in a structure. In *Théorie du sujet* the very term 'offsite' is designed to figure the fundamental opposition of force – these elements *are* forces – to place. Hence an element is always placed by its structure yet also *out* of its place, or *off* its site. The initial contradiction – and there is still a 'motor of change' in the structural dialectic – thus lies between the offsites themselves and their placement, written A/A_p, where A is the offsite, and A_p is the placed offsite. For Badiou this little formula schematizes the division between the proletariat and its placement in the *splace* of imperialist bourgeois society. The class struggle – no longer an explicit term in Badiou's text – is thus not so much a fight between two groups of people within society, or two types of subjectivity, but a fight between one group and a particular form of society whose main characteristic is its hierarchy, or order of places. As mentioned above in the commentary on *De l'idéologie*, within a political or ideological process the split between the proletariat and bourgeois society can be represented in a number of ways – as essentially antagonistic or as reconcilable – and each representation defines a political position. In the structural dialectic Badiou terms such representations the moment of *determination* by place – written $A_p(A,A_p)$ – of which there are two possible outcomes: either a simple repetition of the placement itself, written $A_p(A_p)$, which leads to a dead end; or the offsite emerges through the determination, but as completely placed, written $A_p(A)$, and this is what takes place, according to Badiou, when social democracy, trade unionism or even right-wing politics captures the energy of the working class and its knowledge of its own exploitation. However, such a placement is not necessarily the end of the affair. It is possible – and Badiou sources this possibility in Hegel's account of the dialectic – that the force of the offsite in turn *limits* the moment of determination by place. In other words, the offsite – A, or the proletariat – can, in turn, determine its own placement by reapplying its force, written $A(A_p(A))$. This reapplication of force – the moment of *limitation* – ensures the continuation of the process. As such it is another moment with two possible outcomes: *either* the force of the offsite continues to limit its own determination by place and so it displaces itself, written $A(A_p)$ – for Badiou this was the process that generated May 1968 and the cultural revolution – *or* the offsite simply reasserts its own pure identity irregardless of the *splace*, written $A(A)$. Badiou identifies the latter as the second possible dead-end of a political process, baptizing it the 'leftist deviation', which makes the first dead end, the sterile repetition of placement, the 'rightist deviation'.

What is particularly striking about this reworking of Hegel's dialectic from the *Science of Logic* is that there is no final unity or synthesis providing the *telos* of the process. If the process is not swallowed up in either of the two dead-ends, its final term is $A(A_p)$, which is not so different from the initial term, A/A_p. Hence further divisions, determinations and limitations are always possible.

The attraction of this dialectical process with its alternating moments, $A_p(A(A_p))$ and $A(A_p)$, is that it is not designed solely to map the possible outcomes of a revolutionary political process, which is rather rare after all. It is designed to account for all historical and political change; moreover Badiou critiques other political philosophies for their limited grasp of only some of the moments of this dialectic. His specific target, of course, are the *nouveaux philosophes*, Glucksman and Levy, who theorize politics according to the opposition of the *pleb* and the state, a little bit like Agamben's opposition between bare life and the state of exception: for Badiou this is to think the field of politics purely according to the two dead-ends of the dialectical process; the leftist figure of pure subjectivity $A(A)$, and the rightist figure of reinforced structure $A_p(A_p)$ (TS, 30). The other attraction of Badiou's schema is that one can apply it to any process in one's personal or professional life and condemn friends, lovers and colleagues for committing leftist or rightist deviations. Before terror is unleashed in the workplace in the name of the continuity of the dialectic, note that Badiou theorizes these deviations as possibilities built into the very process rather than subjective faults; it is not cowardice, greed, cynicism or stupidity but a lack of trust in force that leads to a rightist deviation – there are no deviants, only deviations.

Badiou encapsulates his dialectic of the *offsite* and *splace* in a single formula: 'everything which belongs to a whole forms an obstacle to that whole insofar as it is included in it'. In other words, the split between the *offsite* and its site is the motor for the change of that site; moreover this split is universal, it holds for every *offsite* in the structure. But it is precisely this kind of thesis that is implicitly abandoned later on in

Théorie du sujet and explicitly abandoned in *Being and Event*. The offsite qua force is a similar concept to Negri's multitudes qua potentiality: a general, automatic generator of change. Badiou's premise, however, is that genuine political change is very rare and always incomplete – such as the Paris Commune, parts of the Cultural Revolution, and May 1968. Thus whatever general and automatic change does occur in politics is always, in the end, the repetition of the same. It is in order to think what could interrupt this repetition of the same that Badiou devotes the rest of his book to a theory of the torsion of this dialectical process – a theory of the subject. The first heading that this construction goes under is the problem of periodization.

The problem of periodization

If the dialectic comes full circle, and its result is the split between the *offsite* and its placement, then for Badiou the *offsite* – the proletariat or Maoism – ends up as being the mere product of the *splace* – the bourgeoisie or revisionism. He opposes this circularity with what he calls the *materialist principle of periodization*. Periodization ensures that the process produces something different from what it starts with, and consequently that one dialectical process distinguishes itself from another. To explain how this principle works he turns back to Hegel, for whom the moment of completion of the dialectic – the absolute – is the moment of action, the fusion of the theoretical idea with the practical process. In Badiou's transcription, a dialectical sequence is closed when its practical process bears reflective knowledge of its own history. As always Badiou's approach to Hegel is not to reject but to divide his thought and so he distinguishes two possible interpretations of this conception. The first he terms theological, whereby the germ of the final action is contained in the beginning of the sequence: Christ's death on the cross is understood as realizing God's plan for humanity. In the second interpretation there is an irreconcilable gap between the old and the new sequence: the truth of the first sequence is given merely as the factual condition of the second. A new sequence opens when the previous sequence becomes theoretically intelligible, when its history can be summed up, but this summary only exists on a purely practical level. Take the example of Lenin and the invention of the Bolshevik party: the theoretical analysis of the sequence of the Paris Commune and its failure exists and is effective on a practical level as the Bolshevik party itself (TS, 64). The party is brought to full efficacy through the October revolution, and so it is this revolution that periodizes the Paris Commune. However, it then becomes unclear what position the party takes up in the new dialectical sequence: is it the subject or does it become the *offsite*, or the new *splace*? Or is it rather the case that in this new sequence opened in 1917, the *splace* is no longer the imperial bourgeois society, defeated with the Tsar, but revisionism within the workers' camp, or even the party itself? Faced with these questions Badiou concludes that he needs to start over.

To reiterate, the overall task of this work is to found a materialist theory of the subject. The subject is conceived as a moment of change that closes one dialectical sequence of political history and opens another. Our expectations are thus quite high; Badiou's argument promises no less than a theory of history as a discontinuous multiplicity of discrete sequences, linked only by contingent events. In Marxism, political philosophy and the philosophy of history this is no little ambition. The last work of Badiou's Maoist period thus reads like Heidegger's *What is Called Thinking?*, a philosophical detective story, a thriller.

At this stage, the end of the first argument, all we have are three leads. First, the theory of periodization will be constructed by the critique of the Hegelian structural dialectic. Second, periodization must be thought not just from the standpoint of the structured *splace*, but from that of the *offsite* as force; Badiou thus turns to Hegel on force. Third, the thinking of periodization must pass via the primacy of practice, the irreducibility of action, which Lacan calls the real. This entrance of psychoanalysis is no empty show of erudition: it is one of the crucial steps in Badiou's path which distinguishes *Théorie du sujet* from *De l'idéologie* and *Théorie de la contradiction*, and saves his work from being mired in some Maoist tautology of practice. The third lead ends in an enigmatic formula, the first half Lacan, and the second pure Badiou: 'The real is the impasse of formalization: formalization is the place of the forced passage of the real' (TS, 40).

The real and the genesis of structure

Théorie du sujet is made up of six sections. In the first section Badiou follows the first two leads mentioned above but his results are inconclusive – though they do bear fruit later on. In the second section he pursues the last lead, turning to Lacan, but he mentions neither formalization nor force. He chooses not the late Lacan of the mathemes, but the early Lacan and his theory of the genesis of structure; the paternal metaphor as the individual anchoring of the symbolic order. Moreover he does so not by reading 'The Agency of the Letter' in the *Écrits*, but rather one of Mallarmé's sonnets and the Greek atomists.

His overall strategy in this second section is to identify the limits of the structural dialectic – its 'structuralist' tendency to focus on the static combination of terms – by showing how it presupposes terms that belong to what he calls the 'historical' side of the dialectic: terms like 'force' and 'strong difference'. The structural dialectic bases itself on a conception of 'weak difference': the difference between the positions of elements within a structure. However, in order to even posit a set of different elements, the structural dialectic has to recognize the strong difference or 'qualitative heterogeneity' between its elements and the very space they inhabit (TS, 86). In the terms of Greek atomism this is the difference between the atoms and the void; in Mallarmé's poetry, it is the difference between the foam and the abyss or the written sign and the blank page. In other words, there can be no order of placed elements without some form of support for those elements. One of the canonical problems for the structural dialectic is thus to resolve this strong difference and reduce it to the weak difference of positioned elements. In atomism all that the strict duality between the void and atoms allows is a perpetual parallel movement, a rain of atoms. In order to reduce this strong difference to weak difference, and so allow the combination of atoms and the formation of a world, a vanishing cause will be required, a transitional term. The designation of such a term is the first operation of the structural dialectic. In atomism this is the role of the *clinamen*, the atom that randomly deviates from its parallel course. Likewise, a poem by Mallarmé always sets the stage of a drama that has already occurred; the disappearance of an object. All that is left, in the scene of the poem, are traces of that object, and those traces are the combined words; metaphors and metonymies of the lost object that make up the structured whole of the poem. All that remains of the sunken ship in *A la nue accablante tu* is its mast, its trumpet and foam on the surface of the sea. In both atomism and Mallarmé's poetry Badiou underlines the role of chance, the contingency of this *clinamen* or event. The second operation of the structural dialectic is to cause this special transitional term to vanish, to disappear. Between the frozen and sterile opposition of the atoms and the void, and the consistent world of combined atoms, there is an instant in which an atom deviates. This deviance generates the whole but it has no place in the ordered whole since the latter consists solely of combinations of atoms and the void. The only trace of the *clinamen* is that of the existence of whole itself; there is no individual marker. In Mallarmé's sonnet, the foam – the trace of the vanished cause – disappears. The words that replace the lost object must in turn be effaced otherwise they will rejoin what Mallarmé calls the common use of language; the commercial exchange of words. The only trace that remains of the vanished object is thus the poem itself.

The argument can be summed up as follows: in order for there to be a dialectical sequence in the first place, complete with *offsite* and *splace*, a periodization must have already happened. The structural dialectic encounters history – the work of force, qualitative change – inasmuch as it presupposes it; that is, there must have been a radical transformation in order for a structure to exist. Periodization thus occurs as the *genesis* of structure. Badiou rephrases this argument later on by saying that it is only in so far as there has been subjective engagement in political change that consistent historical situations exist.

This argument is interesting from a comparative point of view precisely because only part of it is conserved in *Being and Event*. The position and role of the *clinamen* anticipates that of the void-set within his set-theory ontology. What is dropped, however, from *Being and Event* is this short circuit between the theory of change and ontology whereby all situations are founded by the occurrence of radical and exceptional change. That is to say, there is no theory of constitution in Badiou's set-theory ontology, though some commentators argue that there are elements for such a theory in the truth procedures.[8] The reason why he drops this line of argument is that again it creates a short circuit between the question of unity and the question of change; the same short circuit that occurred in his reconstruction of Althusser's dialectical materialism.

The opening argument of section II of *Théorie du sujet* does not explain how the historical dialectic occurs. Instead it reconceives the structural dialectic as a deviation or restriction of the historical dialectic, a deviation that conceals the necessity of an initial strong difference and vanishing cause. Badiou's critique of the structural dialectic thus adopts the strategy of genealogy: he envelops it in a prior dialectic, the historical. In *Being and Event* he will classify such a strategy of enveloping as belonging to the 'transcendental orientation of thought', which he differentiates from his own orientation, the *praxical*. In *Théorie du sujet* his genealogy is admittedly quite stripped down compared to the colourful pageants one finds in Nietzsche, Freud and Foucault. Behind the minimalism stands Lacan: the basic schema of the vanishing cause, the contingent operation of the *clinamen* and the composition of elements is all to be found in the *Écrits*: the lacking object of desire, the paternal metaphor and the chain of signifiers. But rather than reducing Greek atomism and Mallarmé to this basic Lacanian schema, Badiou complicates the latter through his reading of Epicurus and the sonnet '*A la nue accablante tu*'. The resulting synthesis is a little uneasy and its stability is not helped by some hasty analogies with Maoist politics (TS, 98). Indeed at a certain point Badiou himself asks whether he is not treading down the fool's bridge of Freudo-Marxism by attempting to synthesize two different doctrines of the subject (TS, 133). His answer – which leads to a longer and ultimately more fecund investigation of Lacan – is very simple: it is not a matter of reconciling two theories, but of the real. The real of psychoanalysis is that there are two sexes and no sexual relation. The real of Marxism is that there are two classes and no social relation, only antagonism. In Badiou's interpretation of Lacan, the 'real' designates a non-substantial part of reality that plays a role in structuring society, but is completely opaque and gives rise to conflicting interpretations. The real is something that both causes dysfunction and subverts any attempts to cover over or resolve such dysfunction. In the context of the psycho-analytic clinic, dysfunction occurs in an analysand's life as a symptom that causes suffering. The cause of a symptom is unconscious enjoy-ment: the work of analysis consists in bringing to the surface – through free association – signifiers that are attached to this enjoyment. Lacan's laconic formula for the speaking cure is thus 'treating the real by means of the symbolic'.[9] In Badiou's judgement this also serves as a suitable definition for Marxist praxis: treating the real of social dysfunction – class antagonism – by means of the symbolic order of Marxist theory and party organization.

But Badiou's investigation of psychoanalysis only finds its true anchor when he seizes upon Jacques-Alain Miller's question to Lacan in *Seminar 11*: 'What is your ontology? Take the unconscious – what is it?' (TS, 152).[10] In Marxist praxis, 'the proletariat' is the name of the subject; as fragile a name, Badiou notes, as 'the unconscious'. Thus for Badiou Miller's question opens an investigation into the being of the subject. Lacan's antipathy to ontology only grew with time, but for Badiou this investigation eventually became his own philosophy in *Being and Event*.

At this point in *Théorie du sujet*, however, we still do not know how a second periodization might occur, after that of the genesis of a struc-ture. In the subsequent sections of the book Badiou continually returns to this question, renaming and resituating it within different conceptual frameworks, adding further enquiries into force, truth, idealism versus materialism, a materialist theory of knowledge and the development of militant knowledge in political events. Each of these enquiries furnishes a partial and provisional answer to his question.

Force and the purification of the party

At the end of Badiou's first argument in *Théorie du sujet* he was left with a structural dialectic, the problem of its periodization and three leads. We followed one of these leads by tracking his enquiry into the genesis of structure. The other two leads were the critique of the structural dialectic and the analysis of the *offsite* as force. Before examining force, Badiou warns that if politics is thought via the category of force alone, this leads to leftist terrorism in politics and to Deleuze and Guattari's metaphysics of desire in philosophy (TS, 55). To avoid these fates Badiou develops a guideline: in the thinking of force the historical must be balanced with the structural. Thus the critique of the structural dialectic will not entail replacing it with an ontology of force and flux. Rather, the historical dialectic will consist of a supplement to the structural dialectic; a supplement that is no mere addition but a readjustment of the very terms of the dialectic, especially the *offsite* qua force.

Badiou possesses two sources for his examination of force: one in politics, one in philosophy; the Marxist analysis of the Paris Commune and Hegel's *Science of Logic*. In his analysis of the failure of the Paris Commune to create any lasting institutions of government, Marx argues that the communards should not have attempted to 'take power' by simply occupying the existing state apparatus. For Badiou Marx thereby recognizes the *heterogeneity* of the proletariat as a political force. Lenin's analysis of the failure of the Commune results in the following conclusions: in order to sustain a revolt like the Commune, militants must be professional politicians who consecrate their efforts to extending and expanding local uprisings on to the national level, creating alliances with the peasantry and breaking the counter-revolution by means of a centralized organized military response. The party – Lenin's famous invention – is nothing other than the practical concentration of these imperatives. It is thus the concentration of subjective force that is the key to periodization, to opening up a new political sequence. This is the first provisional answer that Badiou's enquiry produces: *in Marxist politics the historical torsion of the dialectic requires the subjective concentration of force.*

But how does this concentration occur? In Hegel's meditation on force, it is said that a force can react against its determination by another external force by positing the existence of this external force inside itself and affirmatively splitting itself from it.[11] Badiou identifies a direct political instance of this idea in the historical experience of communist politics, arguing that it is only in purifying itself and getting rid of its own determination and division by the bourgeoisie that the proletariat is able to expansively project itself and its goals in the struggle against imperialist bourgeois society. The party of the proletariat thus concentrates its *subjective* force – as opposed to its objective quantifiable force – by purging the party of all traces of bourgeois revisionism.

A *nouveau philosophe* would immediately object that such a concept of the party leads directly to the gulag. But it is not just the Bolshevik party and the Maoist groupuscules to which Badiou belonged that continually expulse members and split; all political parties regularly purge themselves in parliamentary democracies. At the time of writing, the French socialists have just expelled Jack Lang for dallying with President Sarkozy.[12] The English, of course, have a party whip.

Badiou himself tempers this line of argument by adding that internal critique is not enough, the party must also concentrate its subjective force by seizing upon the new ideas of the masses: 'the purification of force is the concentration of its novelty' (TS, 57). In a momentary anticipation of his late doctrine of conditions he then states that justice is always new and engages in a short analysis of the emergence of new ideas in science. At this point force is dropped as an explicit term of Badiou's enquiry and section one of *Théorie du sujet* ends.

However, this enquiry is picked back up again halfway through section three, in which Badiou restates his provisional answer to the problem of periodization: the proletariat historically emerged in the 1830s and the 1850s through its splitting with the bourgeoisie, and its internal purification of its own bourgeois elements during moments of political disorder. In other words, in order to generate itself as a heterogeneous political order, the proletariat had to expel its own tendencies to conform to the structures and procedures of bourgeois politics (TS, 148). However – and here Badiou not so much tempers this thesis but exacerbates it – purification and party organization is not enough to guarantee the emergence of a political subject. For that to occur, Badiou declares, the torsion of the structure must be still more radical: the *offsite* must participate in the destruction of the *splace*, in the dissolution of the order of places. To think the historical periodization of politics, to think the opening of a new political sequence in life of a people, we need a *topology of destruction* (TS, 149).

This is the second provisional answer and it is a little disturbing. It sounds like a rationale for political violence. Moreover it is not just a moment of rhetorical excess but occupies a major place in the argument. The *nouveau philosophe* objects again: surely all political action should protect society and improve existing infrastructure? If the common good is to be realized, some kind of social order is necessary! But then this is precisely what is in question in Marxism: if class antagonism goes all the way down then there is no common good; and what is at stake in the opening of a new political sequence is precisely *what kind* of social order should be realized. If one is to speak of infrastructure, in this decade, thirty years after the first oil crisis, there is a widespread awareness that the major political challenge of our times concerns not just social but ecological antagonism and dysfunction, not just housing and education but sea levels and water consumption patterns. In order to meet this challenge, it is the current global order of capacities to spend and consume energy that needs to be destroyed – and remade.[13] In the twenty-first century, destruction thus remains a possible form of political action.

Badiou immediately addresses how subjectively disturbing destruction can be by turning to Lacan's concepts of anxiety and the superego. For the moment, these are mere leads, introduced in order to divide Lacan's thinking of the destruction of structure: anxiety corresponds to the experience of a complete lack of structure, the superego corresponds to the emergence of ferocious and unlimited authority. Both concepts are developed through an enquiry into Greek tragedy. But before examining the destruction of the city in Aeschylus and Sophocles, another investigation of Lacanian psychoanalysis is opened, this time from the bias of the philosophical question of truth.

Truth is a torsion

This enquiry begins with a rough classification of types of philosophy: subjective idealism (Berkeley), objective idealism (Kant), dialectical idealism (Hegel), mechanist materialism (Lucretius, La Mettrie) and finally dialectical materialism (Marx, Lenin, Mao, Badiou). Each label is attributed according to how a philosopher thinks of the relationship between thought and being. This relationship is constructed in what Badiou calls 'the process of knowledge'. Because this process takes different shapes and orientations Badiou speaks of a 'topology' of knowledge, a study of the frontiers of thought, of its exterior and its interior. Each philosophy thus possesses its own topology of knowledge and a corresponding figure of truth. In subjective idealism there is no exterior to thought, and so truth is thought as *coherence*, as the agreement or adequation of thought to itself. In objective idealism there is an exterior to thought but it remains unknowable and so truth is also coherence for Kant. In dialectical idealism there is a circulation between thought and being and truth is the unfolding of the whole.

Here Badiou interrupts his taxonomy and asks how local instances of truth connect up to a global or total truth – not only in Hegel, but also in mathematics – and suggests that truth can be thought as a surface, a function, and a space, providing us with a tantalizing glimpse of how mathematics could expand the philosophical imagination.

The taxonomy continues: in mechanist materialism, true knowledge requires transport of something from its original context to another part of the same general mechanism, hence the figure of truth as repetition. Dialectical materialism distinguishes thought from being, stipulates that the process of knowledge starts in being, and models that process as a spiral in that it involves repetition but results in new knowledge. The corresponding figure of truth is torsion. Drawing his inspiration from the Maoist theme of the battle of old and new ideas Badiou concludes that *all truth is new*. This thesis will become a cornerstone of his philosophy.

These four philosophical figures of truth – coherence, repetition, totality, torsion – are then fed back into Lacanian psychoanalysis and instances of each of them are found. This procedure is especially important with regard to truth as torsion because it confirms Badiou's intuition that it is possible to think truth in such a manner. At this stage of the argument one might expect a critique of the three other figures of truth because they are bound to opposing types of philosophy. What Badiou actually does, and in this he is true to his Hegelian heritage, is integrate each of these figures as a necessary part of the historical dialectic: Marxism, he declares, must think truth in each of these four ways. And in a provocative interpellation he gives permission to skip to the end of the book to any reader who can integrate the four figures of truth into a coherent schema – on the condition that they are also currently engaged in political activism!

The enquiry into truth does not furnish another answer to the problem of periodization; it simply renames it. At this stage we know that periodization – or torsion – occurs through a subjective concentration of force and the destruction of the order of placement.

Courage and justice

Badiou begins his examination of tragedy armed with the Lacanian concepts that correspond to the destruction of structure: anxiety and the superego. In the psychoanalytic clinic, anxiety for Lacan is always a revelatory sign; a sign of the analysand's submergence in a situation in which the symbolic order itself is lacking. For Badiou anxiety thus designates a state in which structure is absent and that absence is registered as dispersion and chaos. The superego, on the other hand, is an instance that both promulgates the law in the form of commandments or imperatives – 'you must . . .!', 'you should . . .!' – and goes beyond the law by revealing the blind, senseless repetition of its commands.

But anxiety and the superego are not the final words of psychoanalysis when it comes to analysing a moment in which the identity of the law is at stake. In *Seminar I* Lacan raises the question of the end of analysis. During the process of an analysis unconscious and 'anxiety-provoking' desires emerge. It is by recognizing such desires as his or her own and integrating them into his or her symbolic world that a subject can bring their analysis to an end. Lacan then qualifies this formulation by adding that it is difficult to determine when this process of integration comes to an end. Indeed, he asks if it might not be necessary 'to extend analytic intervention to the point of becoming one of those fundamental dialogues on justice and courage, in the great dialectical tradition'.[14] Badiou takes Lacan's suggestion and turns it into a whole new conceptual development: courage and justice will be theorized as configurations of the subject that may emerge – like anxiety and the superego – in moments of disorder. Courage is the inverse of anxiety: in the midst of the dissolution of the established law it designates positive and decisive action in the radical absence of any security. Justice, on the other hand, names the expansion of the symbolic order in order to incorporate elements that could not previously be registered by it. Justice thus names the possibility of what is not legal becoming law; in concrete terms, non-citizens can become citizens, as the indigenous people of Australia did in 1967.[15] Again, in line with his Hegelian heritage, it is not a matter for Badiou of opposing courage and justice to anxiety and the superego in order to distinguish a pure and angelic form of political change. Rather, if real change is to take place from one social structure to another, each of these four subject-effects will occur to varying degrees; none can be simply avoided. This recognition makes Badiou into a realist: for a Maoist, there is no such thing as a velvet revolution. Sustained and consistent change – the subject as the periodization of the dialectic – requires the *knotting together* of these four effects: anxiety, the superego, courage and justice.

The active synthesis of the four subject-effects is the third provisional answer to the problem of periodization. It is provisional because neither justice nor courage have been developed as concepts, and it is not yet evident that they can be coherently theorized elsewhere than in the margins of Lacan's writings. It is for this reason that Badiou turns to

Greek tragedy and feeds these fledgling concepts through a comparative analysis of Aeschylus and Sophocles. Sophocles' *Antigone* provides a clear development of the emergence of the superego – Creon's commands: it is Antigone who instantiates anxiety by exposing the city to the unlimitedness of the Gods. What is lacking in Sophocles, however, is what can be found in Aeschylus' *Oresteia* trilogy: when Athena institutes a tribunal and a vote in order to end the cycle of vengeance, she presents the emergence within the city of a *new* law. For Badiou, 'there is never a return to order in [Aeschylus'] theatre, what is at work is rather the reconstitution of a different order' (TS, 183). The concept of justice is thus developed from the expansion of an existing order to the reconstitution of a different order. Courage is subsequently redefined through Aeschylus as not only action without security but exile without return.

Halfway through *Théorie du sujet*, at the end of the third section, Badiou's critique of the structural dialectic is definitely under way: it supplements the latter with six concepts: the subjective concentration of force, destruction, anxiety, the superego, courage and justice. These provisional results are gathered into a quadripartite diagram of periodization divided according to the four subject-effects, and the four structural pillars of politics – class, state, law and truth. According to the gloss of the diagram, a new historical sequence in politics opens up when the destruction of the *splace* is twinned with reconstitution of its law (TS, 191).

The diagram, however, is difficult to decipher. Its accompanying formulas for the subject-effects are not particularly legible. Moreover, the *offsite* and the *splace*, the dialectic's successive divisions, the leftist and rightist deviations, have been left far behind. It is difficult to see how they will be reworked in the light of these new developments. Much work remains to be done. And so Badiou starts over again, in the fourth section of his hexapodic work, with what he calls the materialist dialectic of knowledge.

Ruptures in knowledge: the eagle

This investigation of knowledge is placed as a follow up to the taxonomy of philosophy and figures of truth. This should not disguise the fact that it involves a return to the major project of his Althusserian period: materialist epistemology.

For Badiou, materialism proceeds via two theses: the first is that of identity – being is matter. The second is that of primacy: matter precedes thought. In turn these theses organize the theory of knowledge, which employs two metaphors: reflection and the asymptote. In line with the thesis of identity knowledge is a reflection of reality, the transport of a sensuous image from its object to the brain or some other recording apparatus. Yet due to the primacy of matter over thought, knowledge must also be thought of as an asymptotic process: that is, knowledge forever approaches reality with more and more exact approximations. For example, Engels asserted that no mammal lays eggs; however, he was forced to correct his dialectical theory of nature due to the existence of the platypus. Badiou concludes that a materialist must not privilege knowledge's reflection of reality to the expense of its asymptotic progress. Badiou's own example of this gap between concepts and things is quite close to the bone since it concerns an error on the part of the French Maoists and their initial analysis of the post-1968 conjuncture. In their judgement of the French Communist Party's behaviour in May 1968 and its abandon of the vocabulary of the class struggle they disposed of two major concepts; revisionism and its contrary, the 'true' Marxism of Mao and the masses. If the PCF were clearly revisionists, then the Maoist groupuscules had to be on the side of the masses and revolutionary ideology. However, what the Maoist analysis lacked at the time was a concept of the *new* bourgeoisie and its bureaucratic power. For Badiou, the gap between the Maoist's concepts and actual political reality was measured and experienced as a weakness in their political activism. But once the Maoists did possess a concept of the new bourgeoisie this did not mean that their political knowledge was complete: the process of knowledge remains asymptotic. This leads to an existential thesis: there is always a *remainder*, something that is not yet known and figures as impossible according to the current frameworks of knowledge. In other words, there is always a marker – like the platypus – of the gap between knowledge and being.

Badiou then turns to Greek mathematics and its own asymptotic remainders. The Pythagoreans held that number and the numerable consisted exclusively of the whole and rational numbers. However, they also knew that length of the hypotenuse of a triangle is a square root, and in most cases this square root is neither a whole nor a rational. Since they also posited that being was number this gave rise to an ontological problem: something belonging to the domain of number was not a number. This is the remainder of the Pythagorean's mathematical knowledge, a remainder which *inexists* in the field of the knowable. In Lacanian terms, the symbolic order poses that the domain of numbers consists of wholes and rationals; the imaginary poses that all of being is numerable; and the real presents a point of impossibility in which something innumerable *insists*. Lacan defines praxis as the treatment of the real by means of the symbolic. The praxis of mathematics – the desire of the mathematician – thus consists in legalizing the impossible. In Badiou's vocabulary this takes place by the mathematician 'forc[ing] the law of the place' and 'nam[ing] the impossible'. Note the anticipation of forcing in *Being and Event*. In Greek mathematics it was Eudoxus of Cnidus who included *irrational numbers* in his theory of ratios. In doing so he destroyed the previous system of knowledge by 'injecting its asymptotic remainder into it', thus opening up a new field.

Another piece of the puzzle has thus been found: the emergence of the subject begins through an act of nomination that baptizes the point of impossibility in a structure and forces the latter to accommodate it. Of course, this is none other than the argument of 'Subversion Infinit- ésimale' which we met in Chapter 1. The difference this time is that Badiou must integrate this account of the production of new knowledge into a theory of political change.

So far Badiou has concepts for the modality and conditions of change, but not for its starting place – called the 'evental site' in *Being and Event*. In this epistemological enquiry he is able to show that once a new field of knowledge opens up, it in turn possesses an asymptotic remainder. For example, in the expanded field of the whole, rational and irrational numbers there is no solution to the equation $x^2 + 1 = 0$. In 1545 the Italian algebraist Cardano began to force this impossibility by using the square roots of negative numbers in his solutions to cubic and quartic polynomials. In 1569 Gambelli's development of Cardono's work lead to the square root of minus one being named 'i', a new number, first among the *imaginary numbers*. Badiou's general conclusion is that within mathematical knowledge, each site of innumerability 'pre- scribes the possible existence' of new solutions and thus opens up new realms of the numerable (TS, 220).

If all knowledge contains such points of impossibility Badiou has then succeeded in rendering the possibility of change universal – in so far as change is understood as the emergence of new knowledge. This 'epi- stemological fable' – in Badiou's own terms – has thus borne fruit. But it has also generated two problems: one concerning force, the other politics. To start with force, Badiou rapidly assimilates his fable within the structural dialectic:

> You will find here the offsite, the splace, destruction and excess. You will find here justice, revolutionary reconstitution of the theory of the numerable according to an order in which previously absurd knowledge can form a reflection [of reality]. (TS, 220)

Not so fast! The offsite does not belong in the same series of concepts as the asymptotic remainder. The asymptotic remainder, like force, harbours a concept of potentiality: 'it prescribes the possible existence' of new solutions (TS, 220). For this reason, it does not sit so easily with the offsite, another name for potentiality, which provides an omnipresent kernel of change in so far as *each and every offsite*, or element of the structure, is essentially not in its place: the split between the offsite and the order of places is the original and ubiquitous contradiction which sets the structural dialectic in motion.

This is a case in which Badiou's supplementation of the structural dialectic entails its adjustment. Indeed, the story of the concept of force in *Théorie du sujet* is quite complicated. First it is made equivalent to the offsite, a constituent of the structural dialectic. Then it is used to think the historical periodization of the structural dialectic. An enquiry into Hegel's conception of force provides a distinction between subjective and objective force and leads to the concept of 'the subjective concentration of force', one piece of the periodization puzzle. We should note that this distinction marks a shift from an ostensively 'pragmatic' account of objective force where strength in numbers decides the fate of the class struggle, to an attempt to account for the peculiar effect of genuine subjective commitment amidst relatively few people. Force then fades into the background until a crucial passage halfway through section three where Badiou embarks on a typical Maoist exercise – self-critique – with regard to his use of force in *Théorie de la Contradiction*. He claims that *filling structure with the qualitatively heterogeneous is a futile exercise*. However, this is precisely what he does in section one of *Théorie du sujet* with the concept of the offsite![16] In section three he implicitly replaces the offsite with a concept of force as an excess of destruction over the law, occurring at a particular moment of history. Later, he papers over the difference between force as offsite and force as destruction by claiming: 'Force and destruction. They are the same concept, divided according to structure and process' (TS, 187). It is clear that they are not the same concept: the offsite has to be rejected, a casualty of Badiou's enquiries. It is a remainder of Badiou's Hegelianism in so far as he needed to *engender* the process of the structural dialectic in a moment of antagonism or tension. The offsite was thus a general and omnipresent source of change within structure whereas the asymptotic remainder is a specific point within a field of knowledge.

The second problem with Badiou's epistemological fable arises again out of a hasty assimilation: he simply transfers 'naming the impossible remainder of knowledge' into the sphere of politics. The context is the

Leninist party and the Bolsheviks' practical knowledge of the state/ revolution contradiction, evidenced by their successful seizures of state power in Russia, China, Albania, Korea and Yugoslavia. Badiou argues that the asymptotic remainder of this knowledge was the transition to communism, given that the Leninist parties slowly transformed into a bourgeois state apparatus that oppressed the people so demonstrating their incapacity to *think* never mind put into practice what Marx had prescribed as the 'withering away' of the state. It is this last task that forms the point of impossibility for the Leninist party. What, in turn, periodized this Bolshevik sequence and brought a new politics to light was the Chinese cultural revolution, the Maoist revolution, which Badiou describes in the following prescriptive terms:

> What was constrained by the State/Revolution contradiction must be destroyed and reconstituted by the *historical nomination of its remainder*, which is relative to the State/communism contradiction. (TS, 222, my italics)

That the starting point of change in a particular political field can be localized is a great advance in the fleshing out of the historical dialectic. However, that political change *begin* purely through the nomination of something that is politically impossible is a little steep. Of course, Badiou also speaks of reconstitution as part of political change but the *only* concept we dispose of so far for the beginning of such transformation is this naming of the impossible. It is at this point that Badiou's theory of change is at its most voluntarist and idealist. It seems that he has imported wholesale the Lacan's early conception of full speech as the antidote to neurosis through the naming of repressed signifiers. Nomination alone is enough to initiate the unravelling of the political order: this is the theory of change as puncture, the withering balloon model of change. It is light years away from the Badiou of forcing in *Being and Event*, a theory that allows for the possibility of error and losing the way and schematizes an accumulative and never-ending process of transformation.

I call this voluntarist and idealist tendency in Badiou's thinking of change the *voice of the eagle*. It is the eagle speaking when Badiou claims that the subject emerges in excess of the law and as the destruction of social structure.[17] It is the eagle speaking when Badiou claims that a punctual naming of the impossible instantly opens up a new realm of possibility. But the eagle is not the only voice to be heard in Badiou's theory of change. When one digs deeper into real context for the materialist dialectic of knowledge – not Greek mathematics but *Marxist politics* – one meets quite a different animal.

Political history and the militant's knowledge: the old mole

The great European proletarian uprisings of 1830, 1848 and 1870 were crushed by imperialist bourgeois forces. For the Marxists these defeats raised the problem of proletarian organization and defence. Lenin, as mentioned above, solved this problem with his invention of the centralized party. Throughout *Théorie du sujet* Badiou continues to analyse revolutionary moments and their aftermaths, October 1917 and May 1968, in terms of the concepts and organizational forms the militants possessed at the time. He thus analyses political practice in terms of knowledge rather than in terms of power or efficacy. Mao initiated this approach – well before Althusser's work on change in knowledge – in his internal critique of tendencies within the Chinese Communist Party. In his 1937 essay 'On Practice' he elaborates a Marxist theory of knowledge, in particular the party's knowledge of political history as it unfolds: its recognition of dead-ends and errors, its problems, its false solutions and its accumulated savoir-faire with regard to meetings, marches, civil war and leadership. When Badiou himself takes up this kind of detailed investigation of the varied development of political knowledge and the pragmatic inventions that crystallize and sustain it, another voice emerges in his texts: the *voice of the old mole*. It is the old mole at work when Badiou speaks of the Marxist's slow realization in the 1960s that Leninist parties themselves could become a bastion of bourgeois and revisionist bureaucracy 'which oppress[es] the working class and the people in a quasi-fascist manner' (TS, 221). It is the old mole at work when Badiou analyses the 'impasse of the political subject' in the Soviet Union as due to the emergence of new bourgeoisie rather than as the result of some inevitable totalitarianism. Indeed, at a global level, the work of the old mole in *Théorie du sujet* has as its object *the critique of the party*. That is to say, the critique of the structural dialectic in the name of history is none other than Badiou's coming to terms with the limit, and failures of the very organization that allowed the worker to enter upon the world stage. *Théorie du sujet* is his elegy for the party; in the following period he will declare its time over and a new epoch begun, its contours still unclear.

In *Théorie du sujet* Badiou starts to think Marxist politics beyond the Leninist party as a rigid state organization. In order to do this he rethinks the party *as subject*, that is to say, *as* the withering away of the state, which takes place in the modalities of the four subject-effects. But it is not only a question of the emergence of change: it is a question of how to sustain and maintain political change. In the absence of a centralized party this requires a new thought of the consistency of political practice; it is a matter of holding together a process that risks dispersion into multiple instances of rebellion that solely appear so as to disappear. And so here again we find the axis of my interpretation of Badiou's work: the relationship between the question of change and the question of multiplicity.

In a prescriptive register, Badiou will argue that a process of change will not dissolve into multiplicity if a pragmatic synthesis of the four subject-effects is created. In an analytic register, Badiou will open up an entirely new investigation into algebra and topology in search of a form of consistency adequate to thinking this kind of pragmatic synthesis.

Consistency and the historical dialectic

Algebraic versus topological consistency

Halfway through section four Badiou introduces what he calls a 'new metaphor' for the opposition between those materialists who insist on knowledge as the adequate reflection of reality, and those who insist on the primacy of the asymptotic remainder: *algebra versus topology*. Algebraic structures are made up of homogeneous elements that can be combined according to various operations and laws. Topology, on the other hand, originated in the need for mathematics to gain a hold on movement and so it gave rise to notions such as localization, approximation and continuity (TS, 226). Topology concentrates on what is 'close to' or 'distant from' an element rather than on the latter's combination with other elements: the central concept is thus not composition but proximity or the *neighbourhood*. Badiou then redescribes the structural dialectic as algebraic and renames the problem of historical periodization as one of the emergence of topological consistency.

The promise of this new enquiry is that the party as subject can be thought of not only as destructive rupture and torsion but also as a new topological consistency; not a consistency composed of elements that are placed according to rules, but also as a consistency composed of relations between regions or neighbourhoods. Badiou immediately draws a political analogy, contrasting the consistency of a trade-union movement – with members' subscriptions and central-office directives – with

the consistency of a popular front. Unfortunately the existence of popular fronts is not a permanent feature of political situations. In order to
know where a new topological consistency might emerge one must thus
be an empiricist; one must map a political situation in all of its details.
According to Badiou, that consistency can only begin in a point outside
that situation's established order (TS, 225).

Not only is an analysis of the situation required to plot the emergence
of a topological consistency, but topology itself provides the lineaments
of such analysis. Topology's axioms state: *any neighbourhood of a point
contains that point*; and, *any part that contains a neighbourhood of a point is itself a
neighbourhood of that point*. These axioms construct a thinking – whether
employed in mathematics or politics – in which there is no simple inside
and outside. A neighbourhood is not outside or separate to a point it
neighbours. Moreover, a neighbourhood has no outer limit; the neighbourhood of a point can be expanded indefinitely. If a political analysis
is conducted in a topological manner, its scope can thus be tightened or
expanded with no *a priori* limits to the pertinence of phenomena under
analysis. In other words, what is at stake is a far more open and flexible
determination of what belongs to the field of analysis. But this does not
lead to vagueness and loss of focus – witness the third axiom Badiou
cites: *the intersection of two neighbourhoods of a point is a neighbourhood of that
point*. Badiou's gloss is that if one belongs to two different political processes, rather than having to choose one or the other, one belongs to
their intersection. Take a strike as a point of a political situation: one
neighbourhood of that point is the working class in that geographical
region; another larger neighbourhood of the strike is the antagonism
between imperialism and the proletariat. The possible intersection of
these two neighbourhoods would be the internationalism of that particular strike (TS, 238). A topological analysis of a political situation thus
concentrates on the degrees of proximity between terms and their possible neighbourhoods or regions. The strength of this kind of thinking
for Badiou is that it dis-identifies the individual by focusing on his or her
collective relationships; he even draws a political maxim from this effect:
'The material destiny of a subject is to have to subvert their proper
name in the approximation of common names' (TS, 239). It is here,
of course, that one finds the old mole again, down in the dirt of the
details, analysing the concrete rapports and common names that weave
a political situation.

At this point Badiou issues a warning; in thought as in political practice there is no simple escape from algebraic consistency: 'Having to
be the topology of its adherence exposes the political subject – the party

– to a disidentifying angst, from which it can escape via the terrifying return of a nominal algebra' (TS, 239). Here again he insists on the inescapable involvement of the superego in any process of change, as a reaction to the difficult experimentation involved in generating a topological consistency. This warning is left in suspense until the final synthetic schema. For the moment Badiou is content to plait these two new concepts, algebraic and topological consistency, into his other enquiries. And so he proceeds to the division of Lacan.

Topology in Lacan: the owl

In Lacan's 1950s and early 1960s concepts of the paternal metaphor, the repressed desire of the mother, and its substitute, the phallic signifier, Badiou finds an algebraic concept of the real qua vanished cause. In the Borromean knots of the 1970s he finds topology of course since Lacan himself had turned to the latter to model clinical structures. More specifically, Badiou finds a conception of the real as consistency in Lacan's idea of the symptom as a knotting together of the symbolic, the imaginary and the real. Consistency was explicitly one of Lacan's own concerns:

> If I use the knot it is because *in* these three somethings that I have originally contributed – the symbolic, the imaginary and the real – what is at stake is the same consistency. It is for this reason that I have produced the Borromean knot: to account for my own practice. Isolating consistency as such: no one has ever done that. Me, I have isolated it, and I give it to you to illustrate it – the cord.[18]

The structure of a Borromean knot is such that if one of its three loops is cut, they all fall apart. No two loops interlock but all three do interlock. Badiou comments: 'The One of the Borromean knot is that of a consistency that affects the whole, it is a One of adherence, a collective property of terms. In contrast, the One of the chain prescribes places of connection that separate' (TS, 243).

Badiou thus confirms that there are indeed two different concepts of the real in Lacan: the topological and the algebraic. According to his dialectical method, rather than immediately rejecting algebraic consistency in favour of the topological, he claims that in the materialist dialectic both must be thought together. In short, the consistency of any structure is formed through both the chain and the knot. At this point in his argument he does not examine in any detail how this might be the case: there is no revised theory of structure in section four to match the early account of *splace* and *offsite*. However, the consequence of this line of investigation is clear: not only is topological consistency to be thought of as what emerges in the torsion of structure but also as what is *inherent to* structure. That is, another way has been found of grounding hetero-geneity *within* structure: as in the antagonism between offsite and site, there are resources immanent to structure for the thinking of movement and change.

Strangely enough, though, when Badiou does turn to the question of change in this section he does not examine these immanent structural resources but focuses on the moment of torsion, thought of this time as inconsistency. He claims that if there are two concepts of the real, then there are two possible concepts of inconsistency or dispersion: inconsis-tency occurs when the vanished cause lacks, and when the Borromean knot is cut.

To explain the cutting of a Borromean knot Badiou turns to politics. For the Marxists the masses do not form some unalterable social sub-stance as they might for conservative thought – 'the poor are always with us'. Rather 'the masses' is a name for the real; subsequently the masses may be encountered within a 'historical cut'. What then is a historical cut? In Lacan's work, the unconscious is said to emerge within the cut of interpretation: the question is then what would a political interpretation be? A revolution? The problem here is not just that the analogies are a little hasty – as often happens in *Théorie du sujet* with the introduction of new concepts. It is rather that this smacks of a punctual model of change, of instant metamorphosis: the eagle has surfaced again in Badi-ou's text. Of course, the dialectician could object that the puncture or the cut is a necessary moment of dialectical thought of change since change must begin at a distinct point – and that the punctuation itself must be dialecticized in practice by making the rupture endure and expand. And this is none other than the work of what I call the 'old mole': turning a moment of dysfunction and inconsistency into sustain-able change. But the eagle and the old mole do not enter so easily into a dialectic; they belong to different habitats.

The entire promise of the turn to topology is that change may begin not in a unique point but rather amidst enveloping neighbourhoods or between intersecting regions. This promise is not fulfilled in section four but the direction it gives to Badiou's research is crucial. In the wider context of *Théorie du sujet*, the conclusion of the initial enquiry into Lacanian topology is that justice must be thought of as the genesis of a new commonality. And in the still wider context of contemporary

French philosophy it is this task – thinking the genesis of a new commons – that marks the degree to which Badiou's work is at odds with post-structuralism and its cult of difference.

Until this point it is Lacan's resources that are used to think topological consistency. The next step Badiou takes is to declare these resources limited, claiming that Lacan understands Borromean consistency solely in terms of existential independence, much like Engels and Stalin on the dialectic (TS, 248). What is primary in Lacan's thought is algebra: topology is secondary. And so to move beyond Lacan the weak consistency of interdependence must be pushed towards the strong consistency of neighbourhoods and the excess of the collective. Badiou's recipe here again is force and destruction. He ends section four with a prescription: through Lacan, the subject can be defined as a consistent repetition in which the real ex-sists, but beyond Lacan, the subject must be thought as a destructive consistency in which the real exceeds.[19] In section five, Lacan becomes Badiou's chief interlocutor and object of critique for his inadequate conception of the real as consistency. The main vehicle for this critique is an interpretation of the fable of the three prisoners, presented in Lacan's essay 'Logical Time and the Assertion of Anticipated Certitude'.[20]

The fable: there are three prisoners in a gaol cell. From a collection of three white and two black discs the governor attaches one disc to each of their backs. Each prisoner can see the other prisoners' discs, but not his own. The governor will grant freedom to the first prisoner to step to the exit and correctly guess the colour of his own disc. The governor attaches white discs to each of their backs. All three prisoners start to walk to the exit at the same time. How is this so? Let's term the prisoners A, B and C. A sees two white discs and – in Badiou's reconstruction – reasons thus:

> If my disc were black, B (or C) would reason thus: 'I see a black and a white. If my disc is black, A and C would see 2 blacks and exit immediately. If they are not exiting, this means that my disc must be white and so I can exit immediately.' A sees that neither B nor C exit immediately so he knows that his disc is white also. (TS, 265)

Lacan concludes from this process of reasoning that as soon as B and C start to walk A's conclusion is invalidated since it is premised on the other two prisoners' immobility. And so all three prisoners stop in the same anxiety at having perhaps anticipated their conclusion. But then seeing that the other two have also frozen, A ceases to doubt his own reasoning because B and C would have no reason to hesitate if his disc were black.

Lacan's interpretation, as presented by Badiou, proceeds as follows: there are five stages in the generation of a subjective certitude and each stage periodizes what can be called a 'subjective process'. The first stage is the immobile wait during the process of deduction, termed the 'time for understanding'. The second stage is the step forward by which each prisoner decides the colour of their disc: termed the 'time for concluding'. The third moment is one of haste since the others move at the same time, which immediately raises the possibility of an erroneous anticipation of the conclusion. The fourth stage is thus a punctuation, a moment of suspension in which all the prisoners freeze; however, the fact that all of them stop immediately confirms for each of them their initial deduction. Finally there is a renewed movement towards the exit backed up by complete certitude.

Badiou begins his interpretation by remarking the fable is an allegory of analysis: it tells the tale of a subject integrating their differential mark from the standpoint of the Other, thereby acceding to the status of a free subject. The initial step forward, in Badiou's terms, is the moment of 'subjectivization', the moment in which a subject decides their identity: 'my disc is white'. The fact that this decision and the movement forward could have been too hasty marks the *excess* of the act over reasoning; and it is reasoning that plays the role of 'algebraic consistency' in this fable.

Badiou then makes a simple objection: Lacan's analysis presupposes that each prisoner reasons in a strictly identical manner. But if this were the case there would be no haste or moment of doubt: each would march straight to the door. To explain this claim Badiou shows that A's reasoning, cited above, consists of three processes of reasoning of different lengths; precisely because it focuses on how prisoners B and C might be thinking. Each of these processes of reasoning starts from a possible situation for a prisoner: seeing two black discs; seeing a black and a white; or seeing two whites. Badiou terms these processes of reasoning R1, R2 and R3 and with the aid of brackets and parentheses shows how R1 and R2 are each included in A's reasoning, termed R3:

> [if my disc were black, B (or C) would reason thus: '{I see a black and a white. (If my disc is black, A and C would see 2 blacks and exit immediately. **R1**) If they are not exiting, this means that my disc must be white & so I can exit immediately **R2**}.' A sees that neither B nor C exit immediately so he knows that his disc is white also. **R3**]. (TS, 265)

If the three prisoners reasoned identically, they would march simultaneously towards the door without hesitation, the others' movement confirming their reasoning. There would be subjectivization and an act of conclusion but no haste; Lacan's episodic subjective process would not take place. Badiou concludes that there must be something at stake in the fable that Lacan does not mention.

In Badiou's analysis, there is another set of relations at work in the fable: if I stop when I see the other moving, it can only be because I believe that perhaps he is a cretin and only able to reason out R2 while I reasoned all of R3. There is only a moment of haste if I assume that the other is qualitatively heterogeneous to me; that his intellectual 'force' is less than mine. The conjecture that stops me is based on the other being less intelligent, less mentally agile than myself. It is this 'less than' and 'more than' that indicates the existence of a net of relations that Badiou terms an immanent 'topology'.

The next question concerns the origin of this immanent topology. Previously Badiou oscillated between conceiving topological consistency as a specific property that may emerge at a particular moment of the dialectic and conceiving it as an immanent quality of all structure. In this argument Badiou appears to embrace the latter option by claiming that the *splace* or structure is always already the space of the subjective. That is, the difference of intellectual force has to structure the field from the very beginning. However, this topology can only present itself via the act of the other's step forward: there is no deduction of the possibility of haste from reasoning alone. I cannot work out just how slow – how stupid! – the other is by my reasoning alone. Badiou thus succeeds here in uniting the two conceptions of topological consistency he hesitated between earlier: topological consistency can only become an emergent property if it is already immanent to structure; conversely, although immanent to structure, topological consistency can only present itself at a particular historical moment, such as the 'real' of the prisoner's act which occurs in excess of reasoning. Such excess is the secret of subjectivization; it proceeds from an interruption of a symbolic order rather than from any calculation.

It is at this point that Badiou's analysis accelerates and starts generating new concepts. He distinguishes two types of haste. In one case the prisoner is so oppressed by the stakes of the exercise that he rushes to the exit, ignoring any movement by the others, and in so doing bypasses the topology of differential intellectual force. The result is that he submits himself to the governor's decision without being secure in his reasoning. In this case, Badiou concludes, subjectivization occurs through *anxiety* and the subjective process is ruled by the *superego*. On the other hand, the prisoner's haste could have quite a different flavour: he estimates that his cellmates are about as smart as he is, and so he cannot wait until the end of his reasoning to act otherwise they'll get to the threshold at the same time as him. He breaks this equivalence by means of his confidence in his ability to complete his reasoning in front of the director: 'victory – Badiou writes – belongs to he who can think whilst walking' (TS, 274). In this case, it is a wager on the real without the security of the law, or *courage*, that subjectivizes the prisoner. What will secure his exit is his own reasoning rather than the governor's decision, and it is *justice* as the reconstitution of order that regulates the subjective process.

The analysis of the three prisoners fable generates a new synthesis of the four fundamental concepts: anxiety, courage, the superego and justice. These subject-effects are linked in two moments – subjectivization and the subjective process – and according to one of two modes: the mode ψ which links anxiety to the superego and the mode α which links courage to justice. At the end of his enquiry into Lacanian topology Badiou concludes that the subject – a topological disturbance of an algebra – 'accomplishes itself as the division in act of the two modes' (TS, 274). Here again, it is not a matter of championing courage and justice in the theory of political change and prescribing the avoidance of anxiety and the superego: both modes, *psi* and *alpha*, must be thought as inextricable moments of a process of transformation. This is not another repetition of his dialectical method in which each moment of thought is braided into the process, as I have noted earlier. This inclusion of the effects of anxiety and the superego in political change signals the presence in this text of voice other than those of the eagle and the old mole, a voice that Badiou's readers may not expect to hear in his work: the voice of the neutral and pragmatic realist, a voice that I call the owl. It is the owl who warns that sooner or later change does happen, in social relations and in the political domain, as history has shown time and time again; and in that change, destruction always has its place. If an ancient class system is to be destroyed – and in France it is the bourgeoisie that now holds power, not the aristocracy and the clergy – then anxiety and the superego will play their role in that process.

In the still wider context of Badiou's oeuvre this reading of the three prisoners fable is crucial: it confirms, in Badiou's own eyes, the rightness and solidity of the line of thought that he has separated out within Lacan. It is the detection and development of a concept of strong topological consistency that allows Badiou to distinguish his work from that of his master. And so in his Maoist period, it is *De l'idéologie* that completes his separation from Althusser, and *Théorie du sujet* which does the same for Lacan.

Topology in politics

The second major enquiry in which Badiou develops his contrast of algebraic and topological consistency concerns politics. This time it is not a matter of hasty analogies but a diagnosis of a political situation, and the ramifications of this diagnosis will stretch throughout Badiou's work in the decades to come. He starts from an analysis of France as a political situation. He states, 'belonging to the nation-state is algebraically decided by a code [of nationality] which fixes the type of multiplicity of the French' (TS, 278). Consequently, immigrant workers are legally excluded from France as a nation-state: they are non-citizens. If – and here is a Badiousian counterfactual – immigrants were counted as belonging to France, the law of its *splace* would be broken and one would produce a larger multiplicity. In this counterfactual there is thus both a moment of destruction – a rupture in 'the imperialist consensus', which solely recognizes 'immigrants' – and a moment of justice – the reconstitution of a larger, multi national multiplicity. Badiou identified 'immigrant proletarians' as the 'proper inexistent of the national whole', the inexistent being another term for what he earlier called the 'unoccupiable place' (TS, 278). This thesis is of capital importance: not only is it the first well-focused political statement of *Théorie du sujet*, but it effects a fundamental re-orientation of the Marxist problematic of the social basis for revolution: no longer the working class, it is the immigrant worker. With this thesis Badiou also suddenly expands the political horizon of his theory of the subject: no longer is its ambition restricted to mapping the splits, deviations, cults of personality, victories and defeats of communist parties and revolutions; it now speaks of the structure of its own political situations, of people living in France that are called 'illegal immigrants' and of their impossible situation.

Near the beginning of his investigation of topology Badiou states, 'a rupture proceeds from an unoccupiable place' which is clearly a transposition of his earlier thesis on change beginning through naming the impossible. I baptized this thesis one of the *eagle's* maxims on change. Here it returns but developed in the heat of real political events: guest workers and illegal immigrants' demands for equal rights.[21] Within the dialectic of political history this claim amounts to what Badiou calls the *forceful occupation of the empty place*. This is a crucial development in his argument, and he flags it as such, saying; 'here we have the first concept of the inexistent as subjective polarity for the interruption of the law and the destruction of the whole' (TS, 279). In other words, the immigrant workers occupy an impossible place by demanding political rights without having French nationality. To satisfy this demand the multiplicity that is defined as the French nation would have to expand, and in expanding it would be transformed: like the economy, the nation would have to become multi national. Here we finally have a specification in the political realm of what Badiou means by destruction; neither civil war nor an armed occupation of the national parliament but the unravelling of our deepest political prejudices and presuppositions, the dissolution of all our assumptions as to *who we are* as citizens of a political body, as people sharing if not a common geography, common infrastructure.

When Badiou states that the destruction of the *splace* proceeds through the occupation of the unoccupiable place, and when he pinpoints the starting point of change and evokes a total transformation it is the eagle that is speaking in his thought. The eagle specifies the start and endpoint of change, thus constructing, in Badiou's own terms, an 'algebraic' model. In contrast what must be developed is a topological conception of the beginning of change, a theory of the confluence and becoming-neighbours of multiple forces in the emergence of change. That is to say, change could begin not in a point but in a region or between regions. To develop this topological conception a detailed study of the web of local relationships, of the *texture* of a political space is required: in short, the work of the old mole.

To develop this claim I must depart briefly from the exegesis of Badiou's work and develop a few supplementary theses. From the point of view of the state and its judicial and repressive control of the population, the increasing proximity of multiple forces is signalled by the blurring of state categories. Take, for example, the November 2005 civil disturbances in France. The most troubling aspect of these events for the French state was that its attempt to categorize the protesters as 'foreigners', 'delinquents' and 'illegal immigrants' failed.[22] When those arrested were processed it turned out that a tiny percentage belonged to the latter category and the rest were French and had clean records. However, many of the protesters were what the media call 'second and third generation immigrants'.[23] The French parliament dusted off and passed a state of emergency law that dated from its colonial administration of Algeria, the mother country of the parents of many of those on the streets. Dominique de Villepin, the prime minister at the time, continually repeated 'these people are not completely integrated into the Republic'. The problem, however, was that they nevertheless did belong to the Republic. What was at stake in the troubles was thus the emergence of a part or region of the French nation that both does and does not belong to it. The French state cannot measure to what extent these particular immigrant populations remain attached to the ancient mother country. This logic of both belonging and not belonging is also at work at a social level: as one immigrant worker said, 'look at my children, they aren't French but they aren't Algerian either'.[24] The point is that these children – second- and third-generation immigrants – are French *and* Algerian, Algerian but *not entirely* Algerian, French but *not completely* French. What emerged on the national political scene during the riots was thus a *topology of incompletion*. The gulf of incomprehension – Lacan would call it the absence of a relation – between the state and the protesters signalled that Algeria is still an essential part of France, but a part which *incompletes* France, which *opens up* its identity: the borders are no longer closed.

When one tries to supplement or specify Badiou's categories, he often heads one off at the gate: here he anticipates my topology of incompletion by twenty-five years. In *Théorie du sujet* the thesis of the forceful occupation of the unoccupiable place occurs amidst a reading of Lacan's formulae of sexuation, formulae that set out two different ways in which totality can be limited with regard to castration and sexual identity. The masculine side reads that all men are castrated in so far as one, exceptionally, is not castrated whereas the feminine formula reads no woman is not castrated, yet *not all* of what it means to be a woman involves castration. The feminine side thus inscribes a thought of incompletion. Badiou does not pick this up, but he does develop a concept of incompletion using a framework derived from set theory. He defines the French nation-state as a multiplicity with a particular cardinality or order of size; the expanded multiplicity evoked by the immigrants' demands has a superior cardinality. To demand political rights is thus to assert the existence of a larger multiplicity and contextualize the original multiple as no more than one among other possible multiples. In short, Badiou says, the effect of the political demand is to '*detotalize the original multiplicity*': in my terms, to incomplete France (TS, 279). Badiou's thought of incompletion remains undeveloped at this stage of his argument, but it is deepened further as his investigation of set theory unfolds.

The final twist in Badiou's enquiry into topology is the thesis that 'every *splace* is the after-effect of the destruction of another' (TS, 280).

This is a return to the argument from *genesis* according to which the historical periodization of structure has to have occurred, otherwise there would be no structure in the first place.

But here it is not just a matter of one periodization but of an entire chain of periodizations, each taking place through destruction and linking one *splace* to another. Badiou has thus generated what he will later call an operator of succession; its result is a global image of history as a sequence. At this point it is not the eagle but again the distant and age-soaked voice of the owl that holds forth: what is at stake is a long-distance view of history that discerns patterns and regularities in the occurrence of political change, much like the cyclical theories of history, of the rise and fall of civilizations, or even predictions of the eventual heat death of the universe. The correlate of this vision of history is a pragmatic and politically neutral judgement of change: little matter whether it is for better or worse, according to any scale of values, sooner or later change will happen and a structure will be destroyed. The owl objectifies change.

Set theory and the reworking of the dialectic

What else is there to bedevil any classification of Badiou's oeuvre into the dialectical period and the mathematical period but his early turn in *Théorie du sujet* to set theory, and in particular his focus on the excessive cardinality of the powerset and Paul Cohen's concepts of the generic set and forcing; well before the full-blown exploitation of their philosophical potential that we find in *Being and Event*.

Although Badiou begins to rethink structure or *splace* as a multiplicity with a particular cardinality, his main concern is to find more resources for thinking immanent heterogeneity in structure. He finds just such a resource in the excessive cardinality of the powerset. A powerset – the set of all subsets of an initial set – has more elements than the initial set. With finite sets, the difference between the two quantities can be calculated: the powerset possesses 2 to the power of *n* elements where *n* is the number of elements in the initial set. However, when it comes to infinite sets the amount by which the powerset exceeds the initial set's cardinality is mathematically undecidable. Cantor attempted to determine the excess of such a powerset by means of his continuum hypothesis which states the cardinality of the powerset is that of the cardinal which comes just afterwards the one numbering the initial set. It turned out that the continuum hypothesis could not be demonstrated, but what could be shown, thanks to Gödel, was its coherence with the axioms of set theory.

Subsequently, three different manners of dealing with the excess of the powerset emerged. The first, championed by Gödel, limits the number of sets and subsets by only admitting those sets which correspond to explicit formulas built on previously admitted sets: the result being the constructible universe of sets. The second approach, which Badiou associates with Rowbottom, involves creating enormous cardinals designed to order every set inferior to them in size. The existence of these enormous cardinals reveals just how draconian the restrictions on the existence of sets are in the constructible universe. For instance, it can be shown that if a certain type of large cardinality exists, there are *many more* non-constructible sets than constructible sets among the subsets of the set of whole numbers. As is his habit in *Théorie du sujet* after the introduction of new ideas, Badiou develops some hasty political analogies between the constructible approach and trade unionism and between the large cardinals and the bourgeois state's containment of popular discontent through engagement in a war. But the real excitement only begins when he turns to the third approach to the excess of a powerset: in 1963 Paul Cohen showed that the negation of the continuum hypothesis was also coherent with the axioms of set theory. Furthermore, through his work, in Badiou's eyes, 'one obtains the means for unlimiting the partitive resources of the multiple' via the construction of supplementary *generic* subset and the technique of forcing (TS, 287). A generic subset is a consistent multiple that does not correspond to any property or definition whatsoever, and forcing is the technique that outlines its existence by adding it to an initial set as an element. Any reader of *Being and Event* will be aware that here Badiou touches upon the motherlode. Sparks fly from the hammer of the dialectic: swift analogies between the universal versus the existential quantifier and Sartre on the intellectual's role in the revolution, on the function of the negative in the logic of forcing and then in politics. But like all sparks these analogies fade away and Badiou is left with the core of his discovery: the heterogeneity of the emergent political subject can be thought in a set-theoretical framework as the unnameable or *generic* subset of a set. This is the very premise of the mature theory of change he develops in *Being and Event*.

The discovery of the generic set is also a sign that *Théorie du sujet*, like *Le concept de modèle*, is a text situated on the threshold between two periods in Badiou's work. To use his own terms, the enquiry into set theory *periodizes* his oeuvre: it closes his Maoist period and opens the following period of mathematical ontology. Much, in fact, is already in place for *Being and Event*: the *splace* is renamed as a 'multiplicity', foreshadowing the ontological definition of a situation as a set. Badiou also disposes of a conception of the event and of intervention using what will become one of his favourite examples, St Paul and the event of Christ's resurrection (TS, 143). However, it is only when it comes to the examination of Cantor's diagonal reasoning with regard to the unity of history that we glimpse the potential of set theory to restructure his entire conceptual framework. From this point onwards the following argument will form a permanent part of his arsenal.

The Detotalization of History

The *splace* or structure of the structural dialectic is to be thought of as a set; as a multiplicity with a particular cardinality. Set theory has shown that the notion of a set of all sets, a total set, is inconsistent. This may be demonstrated using Cantor's diagonal reasoning.

Suppose there is a total set, written U for 'universe'. Take a function of correspondence between each subset of U and an element of U: the element is said to be the proper name of that subset. For two different subsets there will be two different names. One subset will be shown to be exempt from this supposed correspondence. To find this subset one distinguishes between those elements of U that belong to the subset they name – the *autonymous* elements – and those that do not – the *heteronymous* elements. One can create a subset, α, of all the heteronymous elements of U. The problem arises when one tries to determine whether its own name belongs to it. If α's name does belong to it, then by the definition of α this name-element must be heteronymous; however, in that case it cannot belong to the subset it names. If one supposes that α's name is autonymous one ends up in a similar contradiction. This line of reasoning ends in absurdity and thus its premise must be rejected. There are actually two premises at stake: first the existence of a total set, and second the existence of a one-to-one correspondence between the elements and subsets of this set. If one rejects the first premise, the universe is not a closed totality, and there is no set of sets: the total set U *inexists*. Names can thus be taken for subsets from resources outside of the initial set. If one rejects the second premise, one assumes the universe is a closed totality but one must accept that some of its subsets are unnameable and thus indistinguishable. This conclusion also results in the inexistence of the total set U: if subsets like α are exempt from any correspondence there are more subsets than elements in U. The powerset (the set of all subsets) of U is thus larger than U, and U cannot be the absolute set of all sets.

Badiou concludes, and here it is neither eagle nor owl nor old mole but Hamlet speaking to Horatio: 'The universe always contains more things than it can name according to those very things. Hence its inexistence' (TS, 235).

In my eyes, the propositions that Badiou extracts from this very demonstration constitute the deepest and fastest running stream of thought in all of his future work: first proposition, 'every elementary multiplicity induces an surpassing of itself' indeed of 'anything that is assigned to it as limit'; and so – if mathematics can think the structures of politics – it is true that, second proposition, 'the resource of the collective necessarily surpasses the type of structural multiplicity in which individuals are found' (TS, 290, 235). Third proposition: there is no History, there are only histories. At an earlier point in his argument Badiou presents Mao's critique of Hegel's dialectic in the following terms: against any vision of a final synthesis, the work of division is unending, every victory is relative and so the periodization of the dialectic is permanent. The result is a multiplication of historical sequences. However, it is always possible for these sequences to be gathered into one History, à la Hegel – or in my terms, as the owl has it, according to a long-distance view of History as cyclical or spiralling into destruction. Here, however, Badiou employs a set-theoretical approach to the thinking of multiplicity to argue that the very concept of a History of histories is incoherent. To flesh this out in the terms of the definition of Marxism he opposes Lenin's 'concrete analysis of a concrete situation' to Althusser's 'science of history', claiming that the latter is obsolete since 'there is no such object' (TS, 233).

The difficulty of assimilating the thesis of the incoherency of a concept of History is immediately signalled by Badiou's evocation of 'the four great contradictions of the contemporary world' which he held to be those 'between the proletariat and the bourgeoisie, imperialism and dominated peoples, between different imperialist states and between imperialist and socialist states' (TS, 233). If the thesis of the absence of a single world history were taken to its logical limit, one would not be able to so easily enumerate a finite list of 'global contradictions'. Badiou equivocates by claiming that these global contradictions do not define a consistent world history but rather aid in the analysis of local situations. At this point of his work, however, Badiou's thinking of what I call *the topology of incompletion* is in its infancy: all of the consequences have not yet been drawn; subsequently, both *Being and Event* and *Logiques des mondes* can be read as attempts to continue this line of thought to its very end.

The final synthetic schema

In the sixth and final section of *Théorie du sujet* Badiou leaves behind the startling results of set theory and returns to the four subject-effects – anxiety, the superego, courage and justice – the two modes of linking them, *alpha* and *psi*, the act of subjectivization and the subjective process to gather together a grand schema of the periodization of the dialectic. The most significant result of this schema is an ethics that consists of directives and warnings for both political action and philosophy itself.

To start with his prescription for philosophy, Badiou contrasts his theory of the subject with other theories by stating the subject is not given to knowledge, nor is it – as in Kant or Descartes – the foundation of knowledge: in philosophical inquiry one neither possesses nor departs from the subject; the subject must be found. This approach is guided by the clinical and political practices of Freud and Marx whose respective tasks are to find and unfold the unconscious or the proletariat:

> When Marx undertook to listen to the revolutionary activity of his time, the historical disorder of the people, what was at stake was the marking out, at the end of difficult theoretical and practical work, of the dialectical form of the political subject as such. The deduction of its general activity presupposes nothing more than the riots of that century. From that point it was necessary to unfold the complete topography of an order (the capitalist order), construct the logic of its faults, pursue to the very end what was heterogeneous, and *name*, amidst the anarchic surface of events, this almost unfindable subject 'proletariat'.
>
> Freud listens to the prose and gestures of hysterics, to the point that in the end it is no longer a question of who is subject to neuroses but rather of the subject of neuroses. 'Unconscious' is the name of such a subject, here again caught in the net of a topography of the psyche.
>
> Although psychoanalysis and Marxism have nothing to do with one another – the totality they form is inconsistent – there is no doubt that Freud's unconscious and Marx's proletariat have the same epistemological status with regard to the rupture they introduce into the dominant conception of the subject. (TS, 295–6)

Consequently, the major task for philosophy within and for its own epoch is 'to resolve the specific problem of the operators of discovery and seizure of the subject' (TS, 295). This, for Badiou, is the work of philosophy: to isolate, reveal and produce a contemporary subject. Although literally speaking this is not the last word of *Théorie du sujet*, logically it seems to be its ultimate gesture, the end of Badiou's philosophy: a command to search the contemporary political landscape for the subject. Behind such a gesture we find what I call *the desire for hetero-expulsion*; the desire to quit the domain of philosophy in order to resolve its questions in another domain and in a decisive manner, the desire to have done with philosophy and to engage in 'practice'. In its punctual call for change, in its promise of instant metamorphosis, this desire for hetero-expulsion is voiced by the eagle, and as always its usefulness is limited.

But saying 'the subject must be found' is in no way the end of the argument of *Théorie du sujet*. This prescription is then filtered through the concepts of his theory of the subject: the subject is to be found amidst a revolt, and it is the emergence of courage and justice as the reconstitution of a new order that will signal its presence. That is to say, the subject is not a simple entity, but a complex procedure, a particular interweaving of what Badiou terms the two subjective processes: the *psi* or algebraic process which links anxiety to the superego, and the *alpha* or topological process that binds courage to justice. Such a find thus requires an analysis of the modality of political change: not all processes of transformation that affect the political sphere will imply the emergence of a subject. To find these rare subjects, Badiou suggests 'you need the arid, clarified work of a clinical analysis or political analysis' (TS, 296). In other words, the work of the old mole!

As the very *beginning* of such an analysis Badiou develops this conception of two interwoven subjective processes by feeding them back through Marxism's political concepts: party, class struggle, dictatorship of the proletariat and communism. The result, in which the class struggle becomes 'war-insurrection', is the following table:

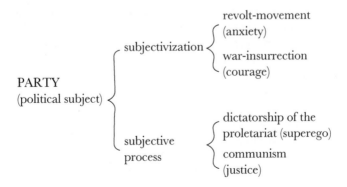

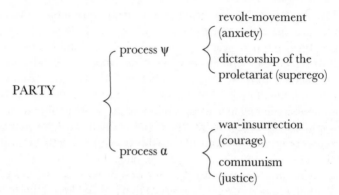

In a further layer of complexity, Badiou claims that the subject is not to be found in one table or another but rather in the passage from one to another. It is precisely this insistence on the subject lying *between* and as a *synthesis* of the categories of analysis – whether those categories be the subject-effects, the processes ψ or α, or these tables – which is the first step in Badiou's ethics. Not only must each and every one of these categories be involved if one is to be able to speak of a political subject in an analysis, but within the sphere of political action itself *Badiou's prescription is synthesis*: to steer a line between the rightist and the leftist deviation all categories must be accepted and mobilized. The question is whether this call for synthesis represents the emergence of a moderate theory of change – and moderation is hardly part of Badiou's public persona! – or rather a neutral and pragmatic vision of how political change actually happens.

To answer this question let's start with a paradox concerning the direction of the party and its tactics. In the Maoist conception of Marxist politics the edification of the party requires what is called the 'mass line' in organization. The problem is that this directive can be interpreted in two different manners. The first sees it as the instance of direct democracy in the party, as an antidote to the potentially ossified and hidebound hierarchies of party institutions; the mass line means that the party must listen to the masses and the grass-roots activists when it determines its tactics. The other way of interpreting the directive is that the party itself must develop a line on the masses in order to orientate, channel and organize their revolutionary energy such that it is not wasted or disorientated by the reactions of the bourgeois state. The mass line is thus interpreted as either the line *of* the masses or the line *on* the masses. Badiou, of course, the Badiou of synthesis, opts to choose neither of these interpretations but to argue that their contradiction must be sustained rather than dissolved, that there must be a permanent oscillation between the two interpretations of the directive.

The penultimate chapter of *Théorie du sujet* is entitled 'Ethics as the dissipation of the paradoxes of the spirit of the party' (TS, 325). To dissipate a paradox is not to cancel it but to transform it into a nuanced model for patient action. This is advisable in Badiou's eyes due to the existence of two possible deviations of the dialectic, both of which result from exclusively following one interpretation of the 'mass line'. The first deviation follows the line *of* the masses and ends up in spontaneism; the position Lenin baptized 'infantile leftism'. The second deviation consists in scorning the ideas of the masses in favour of the security of established forms of political action; this Badiou terms the rightist deviation. To avoid these deviations one must sustain the undecidability of the mass line yet at the same time decide on a course of action: this generates another formulation of the ethics of the subject, a directive that thenceforth becomes a permanent feature of his work: decide from the standpoint of the undecidable (TS, 303). In this model of action each tendency – the line of the masses, the party line on the masses – tames the other and thus despite all the rhetoric of excess we end up with something like a 'middle path' or moderation. This sounds like Aristotelian ethics: political disorder in moderation, avoid intoxication, avoid *hubris*!

Hold together the two subjective processes, avoid the leftist and rightist deviations – but to steer a way between the Scylla of endless riots and the Charybdis of an omnipresent police one must also be wary of what Badiou calls the 'imaginary diagonals'. These diagonals occur when the four subject-effects link up in couples that form alternative subjective processes. When militants engage in insurrectional violence risking life and limb in the name of a higher authority such as God or the Father of the people then courage has bound itself to the superego: the resultant process, in which the individual is positioned as the instrument of a cause, is that of dogmatism. When an author plans every last detail of the utopian society to come rather than engaging in militant action anxiety has tied itself to justice and the ultimate result of this process is scepticism. Each time, Badiou argues, it is a matter of asserting a fixed principle of ideal identity and failing to trust the reality of political practice. It is by means of these diagonals that Badiou seeks to explain those political phenomena that formed the most potent rhetorical weapons for capitalism in the ideological combat over communism: the phenomena termed 'the cult of personality' and 'terror'. In Badiou's analysis, the cult of personality is an offshoot of the process of dogmatism, and he positions it by way of a brief but defiant avowal, squarely directed at the *nouveaux philosophes* and their recanting of their own Maoism:

> I certainly participated in the 'cult of Mao', a bias by means of which I, with millions of others, figured the fixed point by which I marked the courageous overturning and complete transformation of my practical existence and convictions during the latter half of the sixties and the early seventies. (TS, 318)

However, the cult of personality has a very limited place in explaining what may happen during political change: no such cult, Badiou argues, was necessary during the Algerian War for the massacres to take place. With regard to terror, Badiou draws on Hegel's own analysis of the French revolution to argue that it is not the product of an imaginary diagonal but of the process ψ, which links anxiety to the superego: the absence of order is experienced as pure dispersion and a call is made for a reinforcement of the law. In short, the instance of the law – whether it be a committee for public safety or a dictator – then reacts to the emergence of the subject by assigning its excess over structure to every single place: in other words, everybody becomes a suspect. The most significant consequence of this argument is that terror is understood as one of the modes of politics, as a subjective process and not as an ineluctable consequence of the form of the modern state. The left-liberal reader may have hoped that Badiou's theory of political change would furnish some recipe for avoiding the terror: this is not the case. Here again we hear the voice of the neutral pragmatist, the owl: when an established social order dissolves, terror is an inextricable part of the process – all that can be done to ward off its domination of the moment of change is to join the instances of anxiety and the superego to the instances of courage and justice and so engage the process α.

I shall leave the last dazzling dissertations of *Théorie du sujet* on nihilism, defeatism, courage and confidence to the adventurous reader's curiosity. Before concluding on Badiou's passage through Maoism and its place in his oeuvre, there are two problems to consider that are flagged in his argument and remain pertinent today. The first problem concerns his definition of the subject. In this period of Badiou's thought there is a movement from the rejection of 'theological' theories of the substantial self-identical agent of historical change – the masses, the proletariat – to a theory of the subject as that which emerges as the flashpoint of change to a theory of the subject as the interweaving of various processes of change. Halfway through *Théorie du sujet* Badiou cautions 'it has not been said that a subject requires a (sexed) individual for support, nor that it has a (social) class' (TS, 186). Later he says, 'The party is a support for the complete subject, by means of which the proletariat, built on the working class, aims to dissolve the algebraic weave in which that class is placed' (TS, 254). Still later he clarifies the relation between the subject and its support:

> The party is the body of politics, in the strict sense. That there is a body in no way guarantees that there is a subject, neither with the animal body nor the institutional body. But that there is a subject, that one can find a subject, requires the support of a body. (TS, 306)

The support is thus a necessary but not sufficient condition for the existence of a subject. The problem is not that Badiou sometimes says that the party itself is the political subject and not the support. The problem is rather this split between the subject as agent of change and as support of change. In *Being and Event* there is a similar split in the definition of the subject: between the subject as certain types of action – forcing, disqualifying the unequal – and the subject as the body of change – a series of revolutionary musical works, a groundbreaking theorem. The base of this problem is the reintroduction of what Badiou elsewhere condemns as a theological model of change: a model that presupposes a self-identical permanent single entity that initiates change; the agent. The whole strength of Badiou's theory of the subject is that the subject is not an entity but a *singular and fragile synthesis of multiple processes*.

The problem of the agent has a very complex genealogy and it is central to the development of modern European philosophy; however, its ultimate source lies in Aristotle's analysis of production (*poieisis*) in the *Metaphysics*, in what I term in Chapter 1 the 'productivist model of change'. To counter the influence of this model upon Badiou's theory of change, one can actually employ another of Aristotle's concepts for change: *praxis*, action, according to which both the subject and the result are internal to the change; that is, a *praxis* is an activity that modifies the actor. Badiou's 'subjective process' is not an independent and separate entity that initiates change, like the house-builder, in another being. Rather, the subjective process consists of the actual material inscription of change. The problem is that in Aristotelian terms Badiou wants to have his cake and eat it: *praxis* is indeed his model but then so is *poiesis* in that these subjective processes cause a political transformation to occur throughout an entire society. In other words, there does seem to be a separate product of this change: the new political order. What Badiou would like to import into *praxis* from *poiesis* is the latter's creation of a new consistent entity, but without having to subscribe to the stipulations of a discrete agent and a discrete product. If Badiou admits the existence of a discrete agent he reproduces a theological model of change, if he admits a discrete final product he reinstalls a Hegelian final synthesis of the dialectic. For a dialectician, change is ongoing and it is not the result of discrete entities blessed with special capacities, but of conflictual relationships. To avoid positing discrete agents and products, Badiou will need to show how the process of change is not only ongoing but identical to the new structure it gradually establishes.

At the end of his labours in *Théorie du sujet* Badiou thus finds himself in front of another immense task: one that he clearly takes up in *Being and Event* and carries forward in *Logiques des mondes*; to theorize the process of change as infinite, and as the elaborate and continuous material inscription of a new situation or world.

The second curious ambivalence in *Théorie du sujet* concerns the existence, or not, of reactionary politics.[25] In the context of accounting for the incredibly swift erasure of May 1968 from the political horizon in 1970s France, the first section of *Théorie du sujet* argues that one must recognize the existence of two kinds of political subject, bourgeois and proletarian:

> What does this opposition between imperialist society and the revolutionary people actually come down to, in the end? In fact, it is the political division of the people. The two politics, bourgeois and proletarian, can only become real insofar as they each organize the people on their side. (TS, 32)

> The subjective aspect of the force of the adversary is itself still in good shape. This is what forever remains to be understood by the revolutionaries. Many of them think they are the only subject and represent the antagonistic class as an objective mechanism of oppression directed by a handful of profiteers ... The bourgeoisie engages in politics, it leads the class struggle, not only by means of exploitation or legal and terrorist coercion. The bourgeoisie is a subject. Where then? Exactly like the proletariat, in the people ... One must conceive imperialist society not only as substance but as subject. (TS, 60)

However, in the overall context of Badiou's argument this position meets with two difficulties. First, in the construction of the structural dialectic the class struggle is theorized not as an antagonism between two entities of the same order but between the proletariat as *offsite* and bourgeoisie as the *splace* of imperialist society, between a group of people and the very structure of society. Second, the subject is defined as a process of revolutionary change; the function of the bourgeoisie, however, is to maintain the society that suits them, to defend its order against any threat. To maintain a structure is evidently not to transform it and so one cannot have a bourgeois subject. At a later point in the text Badiou recognizes this phrase to be an oxymoron:

> Is the bourgeoisie a subject? I affirmed this here in April 1975. Let's contradict ourselves . . . the bourgeoisie has not been a subject for a long time, it is a place.
>
> There is only one political subject for a given historicization. This is a major remark. Otherwise one gets muddled up in a vision of politics as a subjective duel, which it is not. There is a place and a subject. The dissymmetry is structural. (TS, 148)

This position is coherent with Badiou's overall argument but it seems limited, odd and counterintuitive when one turns to contemporary European politics. What about Margaret Thatcher or Nicolas Sarkozy? Both have engaged in programmes of change that affect the entirety of society; both exemplify an active desire to reorder the economy, to privatize public utilities and de-unionize the workplace. Neither fit the model of the conservative politician defending the status quo. The obvious response is that in each case the new order – private capital – is waiting in the wings; although many social and technical adjustments must be made, *nothing* has to be invented. Moreover, rather than building a more inclusive society, this new arrangement will reinforce the order of places between the haves and the have-nots.[26] Faced with social and economic dysfunction, President Sarkozy's desire is not for justice but that 'it works', where 'it' ultimately refers to the free market, a *splace* or space of placement – investment – if there ever was one.

Is it then possible to keep the definition of the subject as a genuine process of structural change and in some way account for what appears to be other forms of political subjectivity? There should be conceptual resources in *Théorie du sujet* for thinking reaction, because it is a eulogy and elegy for May 1968. May began in a bang and ended in a whimper: the whimper of the *nouveaux philosophes* and their renunciation of emancipatory politics, their condemnation of totalitarianism and celebration of parliamentary democracy. If the central task of *Théorie du sujet* is to sustain and expand the Maoist political thinking that took wing in those events, then Badiou must also account for the betrayal of the promise of those events. Rather than attacking the *nouveaux philosophes* head on – aside from a brief critique of their conceptions of terror and the imaginary consistency of the revolution – Badiou develops in the final section of the work an analysis of what it means to give up on one's political desire. This analysis and his subsequent propositions on ethics are situated squarely within the frame of Lacan's ethics. Lacan opposes one ethical imperative – *do not give up on your desire!* – to society's demand upon its members to engage in the 'service of goods'. In Badiou's analysis one cedes on a political desire always in the name of some good; this good necessarily forms part of the ordered space of placement that is bourgeois society, whether the good be the supposed 'freedom' of the democratic citizen or the 'security' of the family. However, this means that to cede is to cease to be a subject and to become part of the *splace*. It would appear that for Badiou the moment of reaction – ceding – entails the self-abrogation of the subject: hence there is no reactive subject.

But this is to conclude too hastily. Badiou rounds off this passage with a theorem that states that one always cedes on one's subjectivization in the name of an ancient subjective process: parliamentary democracy and the rights of the individual citizen evidently make up part of the subjective process of the French Revolution. Badiou thus introduces a kind of loop or short circuit between sequences of the dialectic whereby the reactive subject does not deny the existence of political change but reasserts the primacy and lasting legitimacy of an earlier historical movement. Another related theorem states 'ceding is *necessary* because every subject includes the process ψ. Ethics is possible because every subject includes the process α' (TS, 327). This is odd because it seems to make reaction into *part* of the subject. What is going on? The process ψ links anxiety to the superego. We already know that Badiou assigns the phenomena of the terror to the process ψ. In fact, he is now going to assign another massive political phenomenon to this process, a phenomenon that prefigured the death-knell of communism in the twentieth century: Stalin's show trials and purges of the party. In the passage following this odd theorem Badiou drops the analysis of the renegade as reactionary subject – for that development we must await *Logiques des mondes*. What he pursues is an analysis of the relation between the *state* as communist party – in Russia and China – and the supposed 'renegade' of the show trials. This is an analysis of the *party qua reaction*, of the party ceding on its own political desire and giving way to the emergence of a new bureaucratic bourgeoisie (TS, 212, 245–6). Indeed it is in the pages on the trial of Nikolai Bukharin that the critique of the party, of its ossification and capture by the objectivity of the state, reaches its highpoint. This is the bone of contention at the heart of *Théorie du sujet* and its final thesis: to sustain and expand the Maoist political thinking of May 1968 one must critique the bureaucratization of the party; politics endures not as structure, but as the historical periodization of structure, as subjective process, as the interweaving and maintenance of *all* the subject effects: anxiety, the superego *and* courage *and* justice. The only concept of the Party which Badiou will entertain is that of a flexible support for the subjective process that is communism; in other words, the party as 'future director of its own abrogation' (TS, 263).

I will end this long résumé and commentary on the argument of *Théorie du sujet* by insisting, one last time, on its universal ambition. Halfway through Badiou declares that his concept of the subject as revolution 'reworks nothing less than . . . any practical apperception of the social bond' (TS, 153). In Kant's lexicon, *transcendental* apperception refers to the original unity of self-consciousness that founds the unity of experience. Let's hazard that *practical* apperception refers to the actual reflexive consciousness of social unity within a political practice. Badiou claims his concept of the subject is at work in *any* such apperception; thus, in my interpretation, in any political practice, reactive or proletarian. In other words, although Badiou insists on the rarity of the subject, and his historical examples are few, he is not painting a picture of long periods of structural stagnation interrupted by brief historicizing explosions. The historicization of a political structure is itself a slow process that is culturally reorganizing both progressive and conservative political practices. And it is precisely this slow reorganization of the structure of a situation – the territory of the old mole – that will form the object of Badiou's enquiries in *Being and Event* and *Logiques des mondes*.

Chapter 3

Set-theory Ontology and the Modelling of Change

Introduction: the subtraction of Maoism

Le concept de modèle and *Théorie du sujet* are texts that stand on a threshold in Badiou's work: they close one period and open the next. *Being and Event*, in contrast, is a work that stands squarely in the middle of its own period, which is the period of set-theory ontology, events, generic truth procedures and the conditioning of philosophy. However, in the previous chapter we saw that *Théorie du sujet* contains almost all of *Being and Event* in germ form: set-theory ontology, the event and the intervention (TS, 143), the generic set (TS, 287), forcing (TS, 219) and Badiou's favourite instances of the four conditions: poetry, psychoanalysis, mathematics and revolutions. Is *Being and Event* then simply a philosophical development and systematization of these as yet infant insights? What does it add? There is in fact a substantial gulf between *Being and Event* and *Théorie du sujet*, and this gulf is due not to what Badiou adds but to what he takes away. What he *subtracts* is the entire Marxist framework for the analysis of politics and history: he no longer speaks of a dialectical process of history, of the party, of proletarian ideology or contradiction. In 1985, three years before the publication of *Being and Event*, Badiou pronounces the crisis of Marxism complete; its objective referents, whether socialist states or struggles for national liberation, are destitute. At the same time he systematically refuses each of the options that political philosophy lays before him at that time: a renovated critique of political economy or a defence of democracy against totalitarianism. The crisis of Marxism is part of a much larger crisis that he names, along with Jean-Luc Nancy and Philippe Lacoue-Labarthe, 'the retreat of the political'. What remains, after this retreat, is the fiction of politics, the fiction of an alloy between the instance of the social bond or community and its sovereign representation by the state (PP, 14). Both Marxism and parliamentary democracy entered into this fiction, Marxism to lose its way, democracy to turn into a state form preoccupied with the management of the economy. In the mid-1980s it is thus time for Badiou to carry out that demolition of Marxism already programmed – as we saw – in his early Maoist texts, consecrated to their own obsolescence within the dialectic of revolutionary knowledge. The text that thus seals the almost complete disappearance of Marxist vocabulary – party, dialectic, revolution, proletariat – from Badiou's work is *Peut-on penser la politique?*, the first text of the new period. Without reading this work one can understand neither Badiou's strategy in *Being and Event* nor its context.[1]

But does this absenting of Marxist terminology mean that all trace of Maoism disappears? Isn't this just a case of a wolf being dressed in sheep's clothing? What happens to the methodological prescription for philosophy, the primacy of practice? To answer these questions we need to understand how the demolition of Maoism occurs. The first qualification to be made is that it does not occur through a critique of Mao or of Maoism as a political ideology; and for this absence some of Badiou's commentators reproach him and many people will never read him. For Françoise Proust, cited by Daniel Bensaid, the price paid for this failure to critique Mao is a separation from history.[2] Indeed, confronted with set theory, many readers wonder what replaces the revolutionary cycle of knowledge, grounded and punctuated by concrete historical events such as the Paris Commune and the October Revolution. For Badiou there are two separations at stake here: the first, acknowledged above, is the separation of politics from any figure of the articulation of sovereignty over community; hence the absence of any consideration of civil society, rights, institutions of government, or forms of power. The second separation is from history understood as a grand tribunal; such a construction, for Badiou, is the work of the *nouveaux philosophes*. This, however, does not mean that there is no possible critique of politics; rather that 'the denunciation of Terror is not a radical critique of the politics that lead to it' (PP, 31; TS, 309). Philosophy's task for Badiou is precisely just such a radical critique of communist politics, and the dismantling and evacuation of the Maoist framework is his attempt to carry it out. But Badiou does not stop with this exercise of dismissing any and all of the socio-historical referents that usually anchor philosophy when it speaks of politics: the most important move he makes is to *multiply* Maoism. The thesis of the primacy of practice is maintained – in the previous period this means a primacy of change and division; in this, the new period, it resolves into two theses. The first thesis states that it is only amidst dysfunction that the structure of a situation is revealed. The second thesis states that philosophy must begin thinking not only from the occurrence of dysfunction in particular political situations – but also in art, science and the situations of love.[3] In short, pay attention to dysfunction for it is there that new thinking may emerge!

What then remains of the philosophy of change, of Chapter 1's 'dialectical materialism', or Chapter 2's 'historical dialectic'? On the one hand Badiou constructs an elaborate ontology that is at once more solid and more complicated than the structures of dialectical materialism. On the other hand, instead of the scene of the lone work amidst a political desert with which Badiou prefaces both *Théorie du sujet* and *Peut-on penser la politique?*, here we have an infinite proliferation of processes of radical change, whether political, artistic, scientific or amorous, all for philosophy to think and invent from. Fine, the sceptic responds, but now that he has cut the Marxist connection between the theory of the dialectic and the actual process of change, where does the consistency of this new theory of change lie? Isn't it simply lost among these fabulously multiple instances of political change? Is this not pure spontaneism, a position that Badiou rejected earlier in his career? Badiou is well aware of the sceptic's concern because he furnishes not one but three answers to this question about consistency. The first is that the consistency of the philosophy of change is assured by mathematics through the thesis 'mathematics is ontology'. The second answer complicates the first by stating that the consistency of change is assured by each individual process of radical change, and that mathematics itself, including the invention of set theory, is but one of those processes of scientific change; the form of consistency it uses, logical deduction, by consequence cannot serve in the other processes of change, each of which has its own specific form of consistency. This is another instance of what I call elsewhere the philosophical desire for hetero-expulsion: the answer to the problem is expelled outside philosophy and resolved by other practices. The third answer attempts to resolve this multiplication of forms of consistency by setting philosophy an inordinate task; that of constructing a conceptual space of common possibility for each of the contemporary processes of radical change it manages to think. Philosophy thus gathers together particular instances of structural change, which Badiou baptizes truths, and performs its own periodization of history, naming what is contemporary. Philosophy is thus a clearinghouse for truths: such is the doctrine of conditions.

The tension between these three answers and their possible incompatibility is what fuels the debates on how to interpret Badiou's philosophy. In this chapter it will not be a matter of resolving these debates – over the use of mathematics, over the viability of his politics, over the capacities of his ontology – but of exploring these three responses to the problem of consistency. What I hope to show is that in the present period of his work, it is not a matter of leaving Marxism behind, but rather of dividing, multiplying and transforming it.

We shall start with the inception of set-theory ontology.

Set theory ontology

Turning to philosophy in order to separate from Heidegger

In *Being and Event* Badiou launches his enterprise by stating, 'Along with Heidegger, it will be maintained that philosophy as such can only be re-assigned on the basis of the ontological question' (BE, 2). For the readers of *Théorie du sujet*, this signals a massive change of direction: no longer is the domain of Badiou's discourse the dialectic of revolutionary knowledge; now it is a question of philosophy and its transformation. Badiou's interlocutor or stalking horse is no longer Hegel and the structural dialectic but Heidegger and the philosophies of finitude. The reason for this change is revealed at the beginning of the text: 'Contemporary philosophical "ontology" is entirely dominated by the name of Heidegger', who also happens to be 'the last universally recognizable philosopher' (BE, 9, 1). These are highly contestable claims! It seems that Badiou starts his great work of synthesis, his system, with a divisive polemic. But these claims are less polemical if we restrict them to philosophy in France, and if we detect their target; the eminently Heideggerean philosophies of finitude found in Jean-Luc Nancy's *La communauté désoeuvrée* and Philippe Lacoue-Labarthe's *La fiction du politique*, both of which appeared roughly contemporaneously with *L'être et l'événement*.[4]

In any case, Badiou uses Heidegger to mark out his own fundamental problematic which is to think being without succumbing to its metaphysical capture in the form of the One, a capture expressed succinctly in Leibniz's maxim: 'what is not *a* being is not a *being*'.[5] For Badiou, this is the same task as that announced by Heidegger when he declares that being must be thought of otherwise than in the form of the object, or when he says 'The Being of entities "is" not an entity'.[6] Heidegger argues that metaphysics inaugurates a 'forgetting of be-ing' behind the fixed cut-out of the Platonic idea or the modern object – in Badiou's terms this 'forgetting' is neither philosophical or historical but structural; it is the counting of being for one, its unification (CT, 25). Thus being must be thought as *prior* to this counting, that is, as a pure or non-unified multiplicity.

Badiou employs Heidegger to anchor the discourse of ontology and to mark out its task: to think being as pure multiplicity; that is to say, prior to any unification into a One, as a multiple of multiples. As Badiou examines this task and identifies its consequences for the nature of ontology, he gradually marks his distance from Heidegger. To follow his path, let's start with the classic ontological question 'what is there?' To philosophy's various responses – 'substances', 'monads', 'states of affairs' – Badiou would add 'presented multiplicities'. A presented multiplicity, or situation, for Badiou, is a counting-for-one, an operation. In other words a situation is not originally one but multiple; the unity which allows us to speak of *a* situation is the result of this counting-as-one.[7] Each situation thus has two aspects: on the one hand, as a result of this operation, it is a consistent unified multiplicity composed of unified multiples; on the other hand, its status 'prior' to the operation is that of an inconsistent or pure multiplicity. This internal contrast between consistent and inconsistent multiplicities resembles the *Théorie du sujet* distinction between the *offsite* in itself, and the *offsite* as placed by the structure. At this point the 'great temptation' arises, which is to declare that ontology itself is an exceptional discourse in that it has direct access to the being, the inconsistent multiplicity, of all other beings. Badiou names negative theology as an enterprise that gives in to this temptation; however, his real target is Heidegger on poetic saying as neighbour to the saying of being. Hegel's enterprise of absolute knowledge would be a less complicated target in that it positions itself clearly as a totalization of all other beings through a direct access to their being. Against this temptation, Badiou posits – first thesis – that ontology itself is a situation, a presentation of being, subject to its own count-for-one. Thus ontology's problem is that of presenting inconsistent multiplicity while being itself a consistent multiplicity, on pain of falling apart. Curiously this is exactly the same problem as the Maoist challenge of steering between spontaneism and dogmatism in assuring the coherence of political rebellion.

Ontology's own structure, its own count-for-one, unifies everything that it presents; being is thus rendered equivalent to the one, and it would appear that for structural reasons there is no way around metaphysics. The challenge is thus to find a discourse that is a consistent multiplicity yet manages to present inconsistent multiplicity as such. Here enters what Badiou himself identifies as 'the initial thesis of my enterprise': mathematics alone answers this challenge; mathematics is the science of being qua being, the presentation of inconsistent multiplicity (BE, 3). And so, against Heidegger, mathematics is neither a sign of nihilism, nor the accomplishment of the age of technique (BE, 9).

In this prolegomena to the exposition of set-theory ontology, Badiou places Heidegger in exactly the same manner that Heidegger places Nietzsche: the announced overcoming or destruction of metaphysics did not go far enough; the decisive step is still to be taken (BE, 9). In the end, whether Badiou misreads Heidegger or not is unimportant – indeed, following Harold Bloom, one could argue that he *has* to misread Heidegger to generate his own work. What is important is whether Badiou actually takes that decisive step and develops a coherent ontology and furthermore what role this ontology plays with regard to the remaining tasks of philosophy.

Mathematics is ontology

At the end of this chapter Badiou's initial thesis 'mathematics is ontology' will be briefly examined from a methodological point of view. For the moment let's concentrate on his explanation of how he came to this thesis. In the Introduction to *Being and Event* he says:

> After studying the apparent paradoxes of recent investigations of this relation between a multiple and the set of its parts, I came to the conclusion that the sole manner in which intelligible figures could be found within was if one first accepted that the Multiple, for mathematics, was not a (formal) concept, transparent and constructed, but a real whose internal gap, and impasse, were deployed by the theory.
>
> I then arrived at the certainty that it was necessary to posit that mathematics writes that which, of being itself, is pronounceable in the field of a pure theory of the Multiple. (BE, 5)

What does it mean to state that the Multiple is the real of mathematical theory? In Badiou's reading of Lacan the real functions as an internal constraint of mathematical invention; he was already speaking of this in 'Subversion Infinitésimale' with regard to the square root of minus one as a strict impossibility in the domain of rational numbers. These moments of impossibility in mathematics are 'real' in so far as they provide negative indexes: *indexes* in that they signal an unavoidable obstacle, *negative* in that the obstacle has no substantial positivity; it is not an external referent of mathematical discourse. Badiou baptizes his ontology 'subtractive' precisely because it is in these points of absolute dysfunction, these subtractions from mathematics' consistent chains of deduction, that mathematics is anchored in some way to the 'real'. The 'real' is to be understood here not as substantial reality, as 'the world', but rather in the Freudian sense of reality testing: whatever proves an obstacle to our mechanisms of wish fulfilment, or our fantasy of reality, is real.

There is a strange conversion of impossibility into necessity at work here in this use of the term 'real'. In so far as mathematical invention is forced to work around the paradoxes of set theory, and in so far as the alternative constructions it develops are consistent, its discourse is lent necessity.

In essays written a decade after *Being and Event*, Badiou contrasts his approach to that of the philosophy of mathematics, with its catalogue of different positions on the epistemological status of mathematical propositions, and the ontological status of mathematical objectivity. He claims that his approach diverges from this entire speciality in philosophy and that he is not developing another philosophy of mathematics: but this is the voice of the eagle speaking! Rather, his investigation concerns how contemporary mathematics might take on some of philosophy's tasks, such as ontology, and in so doing transform them. The latter claim, of course, is the old mole speaking and it may well be true but it does not prevent Badiou from joining the ranks of those who interrogate the ontological status of mathematical objectivity. Indeed in the very same volume he develops his own position as a corrected form of Platonism whereby thought's immanent connection to the Idea, to being, is revealed when the mathematician has to decide upon an undecidable point, a point of the real (TW, 54). Much work remains to be done between the philosophy of mathematics and Badiou's ventures, work that has been pioneered by Anindya Bhattacharya, Zachary Luke Fraser and Beau Madison Mount, among others.[8] For our purposes in this introductory survey of Badiou's work, what is important is the shift in the status of mathematics from the early period to the Maoist period, and now in the Cantorian period. The singularity of mathematics in *Le concept de modèle*, 'Le (re)commencement du matérialisme dialectique', and 'Subversion infinitésimale' is that it provides both a framework for theorizing structural change and an instance of consistent structural change in the emergence of new mathematical knowledge. Indeed in the new preface to the recent edition of *Le concept de modèle* Badiou diagnoses his own early position as one in which mathematics formed the destiny of thought.[9] In *Théorie du sujet* we glimpse the potential of set theory for reworking the dialectic as a theory of change. Here mathematics is singled out as unique in its capacity not to theorize change, but rather the consistency of stable being. Indeed in *Logiques des mondes* Badiou confirms this disposition of tasks when he writes; 'Being qua being is pure multiplicity. For this reason it is absolutely immobile in accordance with Parmenides' powerful original intuition . . . it tolerates neither generation, nor corruption' (LM, 377).

Set theory and its infinite multiples

But why does Badiou need a theory of stability, and what remains of his theory of change? The most immediate instance of change we have at this point is of course Badiou's own transformation of the previously philosophical discourse of ontology via its identification with mathematics, and in particular with set theory. This raises the question of why set theory is chosen and not some other region of mathematics. Badiou argues that set theory, with its paradoxes and its crises, forms a symptom in the history of mathematics (BE, 5–6,14). This recalls the argument of *Théorie du sujet* where he sources the dialectic of revolutionary knowledge in Marx's interpretation of social revolts as symptoms. Here again it is a matter of assigning a source to a movement of thought – or a change in knowledge – and finding that source in moments of dysfunction. Thus the thesis that set theory is ontology cannot be separated from the twin thesis that set theory itself is a process of radical change, or a 'generic truth procedure'. But more on these twin theses later. The reason behind the choice of set theory is that it shows how all mathematical entities, including relations and operations, can be thought of as pure multiples. Once Badiou actually begins to explore how set theory writes and structures these pure multiples, one begins to glimpse the advantages to be had through this transformation of ontology. The first advantage is the ability of the axiom system to manipulate sets without ever employing an explicit definition; all one disposes of is a simple relation of belonging between variables, or multiples, written $\alpha \in \beta$, and a number of rules and operations that develop ways of manipulating this relationship. As a result of such manipulation an infinite universe of differently structured and sized multiples opens up without the multiple per se being grasped in a concept. In line with Derrida and Lacoue-Labarthe's versions of Heidegger's critique of metaphysics, set-theory ontology does not *posit* being as a either a form or object; rather it unfolds being as an implicit consequence of its axioms.

Of course, the mathematicians were not concerned with such philosophical niceties in their development of set theory: they were forced to abandon the explicit definitions of a set due to the emergence of a paradox. This is the story that Badiou tells in Meditation 3 of *Being and Event*. Frege attempted to define sets as the extension of a concept; a set was defined as the collection of all those multiples that possessed a property defined by a well-formed formula. Russell objected that the well-formed formula 'the set of all those sets that do not belong to themselves' defined a property that could not correspond to a collection of multiples on pain of contradiction. If this supposed set belongs to itself, then, according to its defining formula, it cannot belong to itself. If, on the other hand, one starts out by supposing that this set does not belong to itself, then by definition it must belong to itself. However one approaches this multiple contradictions ensue and so the initial proposition must be rejected. That proposition is none other than the one that establishes the correspondence between well-formed formulas and sets. Here we come across the first concrete instance of the real as outlined above: an unavoidable obstacle, a point of impossibility, which forces the discourse of set-theory ontology to change and develop a new structure in order to remain consistent. In this case the new structure was Zermelo's axiom of separation which states that one can only form a new set corresponding to a formula by separating it out as a subset of a presupposed and undefined primary set. Badiou seizes upon this axiom as an indication of the materialism of set-theory ontology: it inscribes an excess of the pure multiple over the powers of language to distinguish multiples. In other words, in order for language to operate part of being as pure multiplicity must be presupposed as subtracted from those very operations of language.

Rather than engaging in a full presentation of each of the axioms of set theory – I refer the curious reader to Meditations 3 and 5 of *Being and Event*, the impatient reader to the Introduction to *Infinite Thought*, and the thorough reader to the excellent appendix to Peter Hallward's *Subject to Truth* – we will focus on the contrast between Badiou's ontology and the traditional tasks of ontology in order to develop our interpretation of his philosophy.

To this end, there are three other axioms shaping this ontology which are important to this discussion: the *axiom of union* states that one can form a consistent set out of all of the elements of the elements of an initial set. Thus there is no distinction in ZFC set theory between elements and sets; each element can be treated as a set and decomposed into its elements and so one. The *axiom of the powerset* states that one can form a consistent set – the 'powerset' – out of all of the subsets – all of the particular groupings of elements – of an initial set. This powerset is larger than the initial set and so one can use the axiom of the powerset repeatedly to create larger and larger sets on the basis of an initial set.

Finally the *axiom of infinity* states that there is a set that cannot be reached through the repetition of operations such as that of the power-set; in fact all series of sets constructed through such operations take place within the limits of this set. The smallest set of this kind is defined as the first infinite set, aleph-zero, the set of all finite numbers. In turn, further sequences of larger infinite sets can be constructed on its basis using operations like the powerset. The result of these three axioms is an infinite universe of multiples, of which only a handful are finite given the vast proliferation of different series of infinite multiples. This infinite universe is homogeneously multiple: whether one descends via decomposition from a given set into its elements or ascends via oper-ations such as the powerset, one remains within the realm of multiples; there are no atoms and there are no definite wholes – this universe is unlimited.

This consistent proliferation of multiples is quite astonishing, and one can understand Hilbert's remark that once let in, mathematicians would not let themselves be chased out of such a paradise. Our question, though, is what is the philosopher doing inside this paradise, or rather, what is the function of set-theory ontology? Traditionally speaking, ontology is a discourse that is supposed to allow one to decide which kinds of entities to admit into existence. Donald Davidson, for example, wonders whether or not one should admit 'events' – such as 'the boiler exploded' – alongside bodies into existence.[10] His caution is motivated by a very powerful rule operating within the tradition of metaphysics, Ockham's razor, which stipulates that one should not multiply entities beyond necessity in order to ground one's theory or hypothesis. Ontology is also supposed to enable distinctions between different kinds of entity, such as bodies and states of affairs, distinctions between different examples of the same entity, and furnish criteria for deciding whether or not x is the same entity at time b as at time a, especially if a certain change z has taken place. My second-year metaphysics lecturer used to ask how one could account for personal identity if human beings could undergo body-swaps. I never found out whether he was in his original body at the time.

Aficionados of the kind of traditional ontology I have sketched here will be disappointed by Badiou's set-theory ontology: it does distinguish between different types of multiple, as we shall see, but it offers no criteria for deciding whether entities we speak of in ordinary language or in scientific theories can be admitted into existence, nor does it fur-nish criteria of identity and difference for such entities. Of course, *within* the confines of set theory, criteria are offered: Badiou clearly plumps for the opposite of Ockham's razor and admits as many multiples into existence as possible; moreover set theory is shown to legislate upon the *non-existence* of certain entities: the set of all sets; the One as primordial form of being, and sets which belong to themselves. However, in the absence of any verification of which sets correspond to which concrete situations, set-theory ontology cannot offer any rules concerning the existence of those entities we speak of in ordinary language. This incapacity is the source of one of the most serious charges laid at Badiou's door (from an empiricist quarter): his set-theory ontology is a castle built in the air or an 'ontology of a lost world'.[11] Yet it is quite clear that Badiou's ontology does not claim to explain reality or carve it at the joints. 'Reality' is not a term of set-theory ontology: all it disposes of are multiples of certain sizes. At the very most, set-theory ontology declares that any identity claim whatsoever – concerning personal identity, or distinct events – inasmuch as it is based on a well-formed formula, *must* separate out its 'entity' from a larger presupposed multiple. Such is its materialism, as remarked above. But then what is its function if it is not going to explain the world or sort out other discourses and their existential commitments?

We begin to understand what set-theory ontology does, in Badiou's eyes, when we turn to its greatest resource for his philosophical disposition of thought and change, and that is the emergence of immanent heterogeneity within pure multiples.

The excess of the powerset

If a set writes the being of a situation or a presentation for Badiou, then the powerset of this set writes what he calls the state of the situation. Every consistent multiplicity is thus structured both by its own count-for-one and by a second count that groups together all of its sub-multiples. Despite Meditation 8's title – 'The state of the historico-social situation' – the state of a situation is *not* equivalent to the state in the political sense, which is but *one* instance of it. The state of any situation is the level of re-presentation as the regrouping of presented multiples. If a situation is scientific or artistic its state will structure all those institutional, semiotic and representative mechanisms that regroup its elements.

Nevertheless, this concept of the state of a situation does provide a permanent structural seat, when one is thinking politics, for the state qua government. This is no small consequence for Badiou, who, as we saw in the previous chapter, set himself the task of thinking communism as the withering away of the state, as the self-cancellation of the party

(TC, 47).[12] Indeed in a later essay he still holds this to be the essential aim of Marxist politics:

> Politics, for Lenin, has as its goal, or idea, the withering away of the State, classless society . . . this could be called generic Communism [which] designates an egalitarian society of free associations between polymorphic workers, whose activity is not governed by regulations or technical and social specializations but by the collective management of needs . . . [this] can be termed pure presentation, free association . . . authority in-separated from infinity or the advent of the collective as such.[13]

Moreover in the same essay he maintains that philosophy can be named as that which 'designates, legitimates and evaluates the ultimate goals of politics', and for this reason it must thus remain capable of thinking the withering away of the state.[14] The existence of a structural seat for the state in every single political situation is thus no small obstacle for Badiou's philosophy. Indeed this is a prime example of how set theory, as a *condition* of philosophy, does not allow Badiou to transcribe philosophical and political concepts into its language. Here we have a clear interruption of his philosophy, which will necessitate some adjustment of the latter. Badiou will remain a thinker of the withering away of the state but at considerable conceptual expense.

Not only does set-theory ontology admit a permanent seat for the existence of categorizing and ordering mechanisms, but the quantitative complexity of this 'state' exceeds that of the initial situation by an unknowable amount. This undecidable excess is what Badiou terms 'the impasse of being': it forms another point of impossibility around which the discourse on being must organize itself. When it comes to finite sets, the calculation of the quantity of the powerset is simple: there are two to the power of n subsets, where n is the number of elements in the initial set. An initial set with three elements thus has a powerset with eight elements; to the seven subsets of the initial set which have one, two or three elements, one must add the empty set. However, when it comes to infinite sets, set theory disposes of no such easy calculation; the quantity of the powerset is literally undecidable. For Badiou, there is thus an unassignable gap between presentation and representation: there are incalculably more ways of re-presenting presented multiples than there are such multiples. The subsequent turn in Badiou's argument is one of the more spectacular innovations of *Being and Event* and it allows him to replace the rather tawdry and simplistic 'leftist' and 'rightist' deviations of the dialectic with a far richer contextualization of his own thought. He claims that there are four major orientations of thought, each of which originates in a particular strategy for resolving the gap between representation and presentation. The constructivist orientation of thought proceeds by restricting the multiples admitted at the level of representation to those multiples that correspond to a strictly defined formula. The transcendental orientation of thought constructs vast multiples that are intended to encompass and order all those multiples that are smaller than them. The generic orientation of thought seeks to rejoin the level of presentation from representation by constructing an indiscernible generic subset. Each of these orientations of thought has its representative within set theory, but what interests Badiou is the possibility of a fourth orientation, pinned to the names of Freud and Marx, which proposes that the excess of the state can only be decided and measured outside ontology, in particular situations, within a process of radical change initiated by an event. It is this measuring of the state that leads precisely to its withering away, as we shall see.

But for change to be initiated an event must occur, and in the argument of *Being and Event* events do not occur in any situation whatsoever, only in those that contain evental sites.

The localization of change via the regionalization of being

It is the distinction between subsets and elements that Badiou employs to develop his own regionalization of being: a *normal* multiple is one that is both an element and a subset; an *excrescent* multiple is only a subset, it is missing at the level of elements; finally, a *singular* multiple is only an element, it is missing at the level of subsets. The definition of a subset is that all of its elements belong to the initial set; consequently, the reason behind a singular multiple *not* figuring as a subset is that some of its elements do not belong to the initial set. Badiou then defines a maximal singular multiple, an *evental-site*, as one whose elements all belong to other sets. Here we find a conception of internal exclusion much like that employed with regard to Althusser and the problem of structural causality, and much like the asymptotic remainder or place of impossibility in *Théorie du sujet*'s materialist theory of knowledge. A *historical situation* is defined as one that has at least one evental site, whereas a *neutral situation* contains a mix of normal and singular multiples, and a *natural situation* is composed of normal multiples alone.

With these definitions Badiou proposes no less than a classification of being-in-totality into regions: the natural, the neutral and the historical, ranging from the structurally homogeneous (every element is a subset) to the structurally heterogeneous (there are elements that are not subsets). Without breaking with his monism of the pure multiple, Badiou thus claims to dispose of criteria of relative stability – or homogeneity – and instability – or heterogeneity. In doing so, he sneaks in a vocabulary of change and dynamism that does not seem to belong in the static flat universe of set theory ontology. The general problem, moreover, with regionalizations of being is that they seem to presuppose a given disposition of being-in-totality that can subsequently be carved up into regions. Regional ontologies then restrict their investigations into what kinds of entity populate a particular domain. Badiou inverts such an approach by starting from his definition of a kind of entity – a natural multiple, or in set-theory terms, an ordinal set – and then elaborating a region on the basis of the sequence of ordinal sets. His subsequent question is 'what is the extent of this domain?' The answer to this question addresses precisely the problem of the totalization of being. It so happens in set theory that it is impossible to conceive of a total ordinal set to which all other ordinals belong: in Badiou's philosophical vocabulary, there are natural situations, but there is no Nature, no totality of the natural. It also turns out that it is impossible to conceive of a historical situation to which all other historical situations belong; and so in line with his proclamations in *Théorie du sujet* Badiou declares 'there is no History'. Thus rather than starting out from a total disposition of being and then dividing it into regions in line with unjustified categories such as 'society', 'nature', 'reality', Badiou begins with a strict structural definition of a type of multiple, elaborates its domain via the construction of further multiples of this type, and then shows how each domain, in its own way, *incompletes* being qua being: there are natural multiples, yet there is no Nature; there are historical multiples, yet there is no History.[15] It is this *logic of incompletion* that set theory ontology will bring to the fore in Badiou's philosophy.

The overall function of the regions of being is to localize change, and not just the global structural change of events and generic truth procedures. One of the acquisitions of set-theory ontology is that all ordinal sets belong to each other; it can be shown that they are universally interconnected. Hence, in philosophical terms, nature knows no independence; there is no sovereignty in nature – this, of course, will please the ecologists who underwrite the social with the natural. Hence, from Badiou's standpoint, any philosophical ontology of Heraclitean inspiration which holds that all is flux – that every supposedly discrete entity is actually a continual modification of other connected entities – does not mistake the nature of being but rather speaks solely of natural multiples. Take Nietzsche's variation on a Heraclitean ontology: according to the doctrine of the will-to-power there is no such thing as 'free' will, only a ranking of strong and weak wills. It is precisely this order of superiority and inferiority which explains how one will can prevail over another in assigning a meaning to a social institution:

> Whatever exists, having somehow come into being, is again and again reinterpreted to new ends, taken over, transformed and redirected by some power superior to it; all events in the organic world are a subduing, a *becoming master* and all subduing and becoming master involves a fresh interpretation, an adaptation through which any previous 'meaning' and 'purpose' are necessarily obscured or even obliterated.[16]

In Badiou's set-theory ontology it is the sequence of natural multiples, the ordinals, which provides a strict relation of order for the rest of the set-theory universe; each ordinal has its particular rank in the overall sequence. Thus a Heraclitean ontology of interconnected and ordered multiples is a regional ontology for Badiou; it speaks solely of the natural – a general ontology must also speak of the historical.

What does it mean for a philosophy of change to declare 'there is no History, there are only separate histories'? Within Badiou's oeuvre this statement stands as the *epitaph* to the Marxist dialectic of history. Already committed in *Théorie du sujet* to the multiplication of dialectical sequences, to the absence of any final unity of these sequences and to the permanence of division, here Badiou embraces a radical separation and possible contemporaneity of diverse historical sequences. On a practical level the occurrence of change is simply rendered unpredictable and contingent; it may or may not happen in such a situation. The only guide Badiou disposes of for locating possible change is the concept of the evental site, the structure of internal exclusion or immanent heterogeneity, which forms a point of opacity for the state of the situation. The problem is that in one passage Badiou also stipulates that an evental site is strictly speaking only evental inasmuch as an event occurs within it. This smacks of Aristotle's model of change as production, and we have already had occasion to note its overbearing influence with regard to Badiou's early conflation of change with genesis. Here the event acts like an efficient cause – the house builder – actualizing the dormant potentiality of the evental site – the bricks and mortar.[17]

At this point, I prefer to install a work-around: whatever forms a point of opacity for the state, or the established knowledge of a situation, is clearly marked by signs of excess and lack. Consequently, one can localize an evental-site without the occurrence of an event. In the eyes of the French state, illegal immigrants are excessive in their number, their criminal tendencies, their weight upon French society; in turn, they are deficient according to every measure of French social integration; linguistic competence, sanitation, secularism, etc. However, if the *sans-papiers* form an evental-site in French politics, it is inaccurate to say that they constitute a point of ignorance for the state: how could they, being its favourite scapegoat? The question is how much knowledge, and of what kind, is necessary to construct a fantasy? It is the phantasmatic figure of the illegal immigrant as parasite that justifies the proud exercise of the state's repressive capacities. The real ignorance of the state concerns rather the social and political capacities of these particular people. These capacities are no mystery; in fact, they form a part of other situations and their states, whether it be the situation of Mali expatriates, or the situation of civil associations that help illegal immigrants. Every evental site is on the edge of the void, as Badiou says, from the perspective of the state of the initial situation. However, from within the evental site itself, its multiple is made up of an intersection between situations, an intersection between post-colonial Mali and the situation of the French economy with its demand for what the ignorant call 'unskilled' labour. In a materialist ontology, heterogeneous elements have to come from somewhere: the evental site can thus be defined as a non-recognized intersection between situations; a disqualified mix which appears, at the level of the state, as a pure disjunction – the French state is *not responsible for* citizens of Mali. For so long the left have been dismissed as idealists but here activists along with the *sans-papiers* are calling for a dose of realism: the state needs to exit its fantasy and enter the real world; in other words, the level of presentation and its expansion via intersecting populations.

Note that in *Logiques des mondes* Badiou revises his theory of the evental site and the event, fusing the two. One apparent consequence is the relative disappearance of the historical/natural/neutral doctrine on regions of being, replaced by the theory of tonal and atonal worlds. The evaluation of this theory, which at first sight appears quite deterministic, will have to wait for another commentary.

It is in this idea of the intersection of heterogeneous situations as the possible site for change that we find the old mole resurfacing in Badiou's oeuvre, and as always the old mole announces prescriptions for philosophical analysis: pay attention to unrecognized but real intersections; that is where thought and change might begin.

The event and the intervention

The extra dose of contingency: the non-existence of history

Badiou declares that there is no general history, only particular histories, or historical situations. The direct consequence of this thesis is that events have no ground, there is no one original situation which produces events and nor can they be sourced in any particular situation. Since events do not belong to any situation, Badiou classifies them as falling into the category of that-which-is-not-being-qua-being. As such, mathematical ontology cannot speak of them and Badiou must engage in his own philosophical construction of the concept of the event. According to the doctrine of conditions, philosophical construction proceeds by analysing the new thinking that emerges in procedures of radical change in art, science, love and politics. Thus, when examining Badiou's concept of the event it is imperative to remember that it is conditioned by his analysis of Mallarmé's 'revolution in verse' in the shape of the poem 'A Cast of Dice . . .'.

The first characteristic of the event is that it is local and does not take place across an entire situation, but occurs at a particular point in the situation: the evental site. The second characteristic is its absolute contingency: nothing prescribes the occurrence of an event; the existence of an evental site is a necessary but non-sufficient condition. Here Badiou places the error of deterministic theories of change; they confuse the existence of an evental site with the existence of change. The third characteristic of the event is that it is undecidable whether it belongs to the situation or not. One may object that surely it is evident that the event does *not* belong to the situation; however, in line with the axiom of extension, to decide whether or not a multiple belongs to a situation one must investigate its elements. If one investigates the elements of an event, one finds that it contains all of the elements of the evental-site – and none of these belong to the initial situation, this much is clear – but it also contains itself, its own name. This is the fourth characteristic of the event, its reflexivity. In order to identify an event and decide its belonging – by investigating its elements – one must thus have already have identified it, because it is one of its elements.

This is quite a neat formal solution to the event's exteriority to ontology: the self-belonging of multiples leads to Russell's paradox and is indirectly prohibited by the axiom of foundation. The event is thus cemented into the category of that-which-is-not-being-qua-being inasmuch as its structure forms a point of impossibility for the discourse of ontology. The event thus finds its place in the overall disposition of Badiou's discourses, but it is quite another thing to understand what this structure of reflexivity means. We shall come back to this. From the standpoint of the situation there are no criteria for deciding whether or not the event is: a pure anomaly; an accident arising from another situation; or a strange product of the situation itself. Consequently, the event as a presented multiple has no anchor and as such no consistency. In a rare usage of phenomenological language, Badiou says that the event is doomed to appear so as to immediately disappear; this is its sixth characteristic, it is existentially fragile, ephemeral.

All of these characteristics would seem to add up to the event being rendered equivalent to chance. If an event does not belong to any situation, it cannot be assigned a cause, and so it breaks with Leibniz's principle of sufficient reason. But this is not quite exact. Conceptually speaking, chance can calculated and presented as belonging to the discursive situation of statistics; moreover, computer programs running certain algorithms can generate randomness, as Ray Brassier has argued.[18] The particular form of chance at stake in the event is rather that captured in Aristotle's category of *tuche* as reworked by Lacan in Seminar 11: the missed encounter, or the irruption of dysfunction.[19] As such, the event is not so much the emergence of a new entity as a tear opening up in the texture of a situation; it is opaque and establishes nothing.

But what can we make of this reflexivity of the event? Badiou's examples are always political; he speaks of how the name of the event – the 'Revolution' – is an active unifying element within the historical process of the French revolution itself, citing St Just's 'the revolution is frozen' as a typical instance of such self-belonging. In *Logiques des mondes*, he speaks of the '18th of March' and its role during the Paris Commune. The reflexivity of the event is also easy to imagine in an amorous truth procedure; the initial encounter of the two lovers forms a fundamental element within that encounter inasmuch as it is extended and expanded through the practice of their love. This is precisely what 'love at first sight' means, not full knowledge or experience of what love will come to mean, but the impossibility of analysing or absorbing of the sheer factuality, the singular fortune of the meeting that brings the two lovers together. The reflexive structure of a scientific or artistic event is not as immediately evident. How does Duchamp's urinal belong to the event that it is in the field of modern art?[20]

The reflexivity of the event implies an original theatricality; it stages and announces itself, it insists within itself. In so far as this concept is conditioned by a poem – Mallarmé's 'A Cast of Dice . . .' – its interpretation can be conditioned by another poem: Aeneas, shrouded in mist, a hidden tourist in the boom-town of Carthage, comes across a bronze frieze in a temple which recounts part of his own life, the Trojan War and the sack of Troy, he even sees a representation of himself amidst the battle.[21] He is thus faced with a representation of the very disaster that led to his current predicament, fleet annihilated, stranded on foreign shores, a predicament that through his voyage and his attitude towards his fate is the direct extension and continuation of that original disaster. The first half of the *Aeneid* is devoted to presenting the prolongation of the disastrous event that is the sack of Troy, a disaster that is not confined to the fires of one sole night but affects the destiny of an entire people who become homeless and are forced into a hesitant nomadism. One element of that extended disaster is the hero's coming across a work of art that presents part of that disaster, the subsequent parts being presented through Aeneas' own retelling of his voyages to Dido at the banquet. Throughout the first half of the poem Aeneas cannot escape this disaster: he lives within it, and he is continually presented with it.

If our own interpretation of Badiou is conditioned by *The Aeneid*, part of the generic truth procedure of epic poetry, we can argue that the event is reflexive in so far as it is a *disaster*. For an event to truly interrupt a situation and cause dysfunction, the presence of its opaque identity must be insistent in some manner, and where else would this opacity be repeated but in attempts to analyse or assimilate the event; attempts frustrated precisely by this reflexive structure. Knowledge cannot process this multiple, no decomposition or re-composition can interpret it; this insistence within itself is what Badiou calls the ultra-One. I would call it the Same-Same of the disaster.

To jump ahead of ourselves, this reflexive structure not only blocks knowledge but also incites it to re-invent its categories. If, in order to know what kind of multiple the event is, one already needs to know what it is, then the identity of the event is suspended from the acquisition of a knowledge that one evidently does not yet possess. However, when one does come to possess this knowledge, one will have already possessed it due to its reflexive structure: to know what the event is one has to already know what it is composed of. This strange logic of the future anterior is precisely that of the generic procedure and its enquiries into the consequences of the event belonging to a situation. The fact that the structure of the event already prescribes this logic indicates that the identity of the event will be retrospectively established through the procedure of change on the basis of each enquiry: this anomalous multiple will gain identity through its expansion across a situation. There are high-school teachers in France who try to educate students in line with the maxim inscribed over the front door of every public school: *liberté, egalité, fraternité*. These teachers are still trying to work out just what the French revolution is, and what it entails, in the field of education. The French revolution is not yet closed. *Aux armes citoyens!* The revolution is not yet over.

But for such an enquiry to take place, and an event's identity to be retroactively assigned, first it must gain some consistency; a decision must be taken as to its belonging. Badiou terms 'intervention' any procedure that names the event as belonging to the situation without annulling its eventhood.

The intervention and the self-naming of the event

An intervention is a gamble that saves the event from oblivion by pinning a signifier upon it. The intervention orientates the event towards the situation, and by naming it draws it into linguistic circulation. In order to do so without reducing its eventhood, the name cannot be drawn from multiples presented in the situation, but rather from unpresented multiples, or the void. In other words, the intervention names the event with an element of the eventual site (BE, 204). From the point of view of the situation and its state this name is indistinct since it does not belong to the situation; it is not a proper name and what it names is thus not a distinct entity. Thus, from the standpoint of the situation, the event does not fall under the law of the count-for-one; it is not a unified structured multiple. From the perspective of the state of the situation, the nomination of the event corresponds to no law of representation; there are no rules regulating this nomination. The direct consequence of this illegality of the nomination is that the intervention does not quell the undecidability of the event once and for all; each time that someone explores the consequences of the intervention they will have to decide again that it, and the event, took place within the situation, and that their efficacy requires further evaluation. As a result there can be no hero of the event; the intervention does not secure once and for all the belonging of the event to the situation and hence the transformation of the latter. This qualification is fundamental with regard to the possible re-emergence of the voice of the eagle within Badiou's philosophy of change, but more on the bestiary later. From the standpoint of the state, an indistinct name has emerged in relation to the evental site and the connection between the two remains completely opaque. Moreover, in so far as it is the state, with its diverse representational mechanisms, that places the presented multiples of the situation and establishes various orders, the position of the event, having no fixed place, can only be that of a nomadic or 'erring' multiple whose movement is not orientated and thus can only be described as random. Furthermore, it is not even a multiple but a kind of interval, a moment of suspense between an indistinct name and unpresented multiples. If the state is capable of reacting to this mobile anomaly, it is only to claim that some external agent lies behind the enigmatic connection between the name and the site: Badiou, of course, is arguing that what is responsible *is* external to the state but immanent to the situation; hence it is not structure per se that will form the object of his critique – as in *Théorie du sujet* – but that particular form of structure that is the state.

Finally, in his development of the concept of intervention Badiou asks the crucial question of how an illegal nomination might be possible given that no resources in the state or the situation could support its subtraction from the laws of presentation and representation. If it is the event that founds the possibility of an intervention, the only solution, in Badiou's eyes, is that a new event can solely be recognized as such from the point of view of a previous intervention and its consequences. One of Badiou's canonical examples is Lenin's fidelity to the event of the Paris Commune and its consequences for communist politics; this is what allowed Lenin to recognize the civil turmoil of 1917 as a revolutionary moment, as a new event. What we have here is another version of *Théorie du sujet*'s periodization of the structural dialectic: interventions found historicity. As Badiou himself notes, in a frustratingly brief aside, any theory of temporality, of time as differentiation rather than as measured order, would base itself on the difference between two interventions. Usually *Being and Event* is read as effectuating a pulverization of the Marxist conception of history as an orientated totality; as mentioned above, there is no History, only historical situations. What Badiou is forced to allow here, though, are sequences of historical situations that closely resemble the historicized dialectic of *Théorie du sujet*. One doesn't have history as totality, but one certainly has a conception of long historical series, of histories that are not just local, but *regional*. Note that the investigation of the power of regionalization becomes an explicit concern in *Logiques des mondes*.

It is precisely when Badiou admits the linking up of historical sequences within a particular domain, such as politics, that a familiar voice reappears in his theorization of change: the voice of the owl. The owl enjoys a long-distance vision of change and searches for patterns or constants in the emergence and forms of change. From the owl's standpoint the occurrence of events is *assured*; they may not be particularly predictable, and they may not happen everywhere and all the time, but events have occurred and will occur. Moreover, seen from afar, the processes of transformation initiated by interventions lead to the production of a new situation, and the features of that new situation are in some way a result of that process. What we are beginning to glimpse here, within one voice or current of Badiou's thought of change, is the spectre of a theory of genesis, of constitution, which is precisely what many commentators feel is missing from his set-theory ontology.[22] If the owl has its way over the other voices, the eagle and the old mole, then a theory of genesis – à la Simondon? – may prove the logical extension of Badiou's philosophy. We shall decide which of the voices has its way over the others only once the exegesis of generic truth procedures is complete. To begin this exegesis, though, we must finish with the intervention and the objections it provoked.

In one of the very few but valuable moments in which he performs an about-turn, Badiou retracts his theory of intervention in the Preface to the English translation of his *Ethics*, published in 2001, and in *Logiques des mondes*, published in 2006. In the latter work he reveals that a series of criticisms made by Gilles Deleuze, Jean-François Lyotard, Jean-Luc Nancy and Jean-Toussaint Desanti regarding the evental site and the intervention alerted him to problems in their formulation and led him to modify his conception by fusing the event and its site. In particular, Lyotard's critique concerned the emergence of decisionism, of a kind of Schmittian voluntarism, in Badiou's theory of change. For Schmitt the sovereign is constituted through the action of making decisions in exceptional circumstances, and for Lyotard this is precisely what happens in the intervention; there is a transcendental agency that gains sovereignty through deciding on the belonging of an exceptional element. However in Badiou's theory, the subject is posterior to the event in Badiou's conception, and so there can be no 'transcendental agency' prior to the event. But Lyotard's objection holds either way: if the event is named via an 'illegal' procedure, then one must suppose an 'unclear transcendental structure', in Badiou's own terms.[23] And if one employs the solution mentioned above – a subject faithful to a previous fidelity names the event – and insists that the subjects of the new event are posterior, one can still object that the intervention thus describes the constitution of a new sovereign; each decision on an exceptional event, in the absence of structural constraints, signs the emergence of a pure will, of a sovereign subject.[24] In my terms, this would sign the hegemony of the eagle in Badiou's theory of change. However, there are two reasons why this objection fails: the first is that there are structural constraints on the unfolding of a generic truth procedure; it is quite possible for the procedure of forcing to come across multiples that are not connected to the event, and thus do not form one of its consequences. The generic procedure thus cannot be the expression of a will alone; this argument will be picked up again later. The second reason is that those subjects that are posterior to event are not heroic individuals, but enquiries and practices that take place *between and through* individuals – a political subject, Badiou says, is a meeting, a tract or a protest rally, not an individual, and an amorous subject is what happens in between two individuals, like moving in together, or surviving illness. Sovereignty presupposes unity, and there is no simple unity in a generic procedure.

But it is not just the intervention as a second miraculous event that Badiou recognizes as problematic but also the evental site, whose formalization, on his own admission, proved difficult.[25] His solution in *Logiques des mondes* is to fuse all three categories: the event is a particular kind of site, and the event itself has consequences and leaves traces in the logical structure of a world. The most difficult aspect of this reconstruction of his theory is again the self-reflexivity of the site. In his new terminology each element of a multiple is indexed to a transcendental scale of intensities of appearance that is immanent to a particular world. In the case of a site, not only are each of its elements assigned a degree of intensity, but its entire being appears and is indexed. In other words, the being of a site – its pure multiplicity – which supports its appearance, appears itself in the field of intensities; that is, the field of relations of identity and difference. Badiou admits that the idea is obscure and immediately illustrates it by recourse to amorous and political examples – as noted above – in which self-reflexivity occurs as a kind of self-naming and in which the name of the site plays a role in its own unfolding as a multiple. In some way, the reflexivity of the event is already thought of as a kind of self-naming in *Being and Event*. Strictly speaking, it is the intervention that names the event with a multiple, x, drawn from the evental site, X (BE, 204). However, the event itself has a self-reflexive structure – its matheme is e_x

$= \{e_x \: / \: x \in X\}$ where e_x is the event, X the eventual site and x the elements of the eventual site. Moreover, before Badiou develops his concept of the intervention, he speaks of the event's 'power of nomination' (BE, 182). What he is referring to here is how, from the standpoint of the situation, the only thing which stops an event from disappearing into the void of the evental site, the $x \in X$, is the event's placement of itself, e_x, between itself and the evental site. In other words, the event does not just consist of elements of the evental site – in which case it can be easily dismissed as an external accident from the point of view of the situation – but also consists of itself. This is the structure of disaster or insistent dysfunction that I spoke of above. If an event can name itself one can argue that the event and the intervention are already fused in *Being and Event*.

But if one thinks about Badiou's historical and political examples, one realizes that a date – a historical name for an event, like 18 March 1871 – becomes an internal motivating factor within the period it designates *solely* when something exceptional happens and one does not yet possess an explanation or concept for that occurrence. But surely the 'Cold War' was a unifying signifier that played an active organizing role in the very period it named; moreover it certainly designated an exceptional period in political history. Self-naming is evidently not enough to guarantee that a site will give rise to the kind of change Badiou calls a 'generic truth procedure'. It is for this reason that Badiou adds a number of criteria in *Logiques des mondes* for the identification of an event. An event is the type of site that has implications for the logics of appearance of its world. First, a site-event has a maximal intensity of appearance; and second, the fundamental consequence of its appearance must be that whatever multiple which previously belonged to the situation but failed to have any intensity of appearance, the *inexistent*, now enjoys a maximal intensity of appearance. In the world of the Paris Commune, the inexistent – the multiple which belongs but does not appear – is the political capacity of the working class. The immediate consequence of the formation of the Paris Commune on 18 March 1871 is that the political capacity of the proletariat achieved maximum intensity and so left a lasting mark in the world of European politics.

It is not enough, however, for an event to leave a mark for a structural change to occur. The question that Badiou asks himself in *Being and Event* is how the consequences of an event can be explored and maintained while conserving their evental nature. His answer is that a very particular organized discipline is required called a *fidelity*. What a fidelity does is slowly outline an as yet indiscernible sub-multiple of the situation: *the generic multiple*.

Forcing and the generic

The existence of unknown consistency

The doctrine of forcing and the generic forms the heart of Badiou's enterprise in *Being and Event* and it gives rise to the most difficult passages in the book. Nevertheless, its import for the thinking of change is as simple as it is startling: within a situation it is possible to construct, step by step, the outline of a coherent multiple which gathers together elements from the entirety of the situation – it takes a little bit of everything – and yet in its entirety it is completely unknowable and does not correspond to any knowledge one has of the components of that situation. In other words, there is *something lying beneath*, or *something at work* in the situation, something that remains to be discovered through a constructive practice. In short, there is unknown consistency, there is a way of doing things – in politics, in science, in art, in love – that *works*, but that remains foreign to our imagination.

This consistency, however, does not emerge all at once as soon as the event is named as belonging to the situation. Rather, it is unfolded step by step in an infinite procedure made up of what Badiou calls 'enquiries'. An enquiry is an encounter with various multiples of the situation, in which a decision is made as to whether they are connected to the event or not. Those multiples that turn out to be connected to the event are slowly gathered together and form a generic multiple, a subset of the situation which signals its novelty by being unclassifiable for the established knowledge of the situation. That is, whatever concept or category one employs to characterize this synthetic multiple, it always contains at least one element which does not correspond to that concept. The generic multiple, in Badiou's terms, 'subtracts itself, in at least one of its points, from discernment by any property whatsoever', and this is why it is said to be *indiscernible* (BE, 370). In an actual truth procedure, this subtraction translates into an endless process of division between the new practices subsequent to the event, and the old ideas and practices that don't quite capture the promise of the event.

However, the generic multiple is not just indiscernible; it is also generic in that for each and every property one chooses *some* of the elements of the generic multiple possess that property, but not all. In mathematical terms, a *domination* is a multiple that negates one property *but at the same time* defines a contrary property: the generic subset is a multiple that intersects – contains some elements of – every domination. The generic multiple thus contains at least one element corresponding to every property whatsoever; it contains a little bit of everything. Badiou writes:

> What happens in art, in science, in true (rare) politics, and in love (if it exists), is the coming to light of an indiscernible of the times, which, as such, is neither a known or recognized multiple, nor an ineffable singularity, but that which detains in its multiple-being all the common traits of the collective in question: in this sense, it is the truth of the collective's being. (BE, 17)

Badiou thus adds a new definition of truth to philosophy's larder: the truth of a situation is the generic multiple consisting of particular elements that are gradually separated out from others in the enquiries due to their being connected to the name of the event. The generic multiple is the truth of a situation in so far as it is both inclusive – given any property, some of its elements possess it – and yet indiscernible – no property serves to classify it as a whole. For this reason Badiou writes; 'the procedure of a fidelity traverses existent knowledge' (BE, 327). It does not take place in some sublime outside of knowledge but rather cuts through and intersects with each category: let's note in passing that this is precisely what Badiou claims that his own philosophy does with regard the categories of Heidegger's philosophy, analytic philosophy and militant or clinical doctrines of the subject (BE, 2). One should also note that Althusser himself warns that the formulation 'X is the truth of Y', where X and Y are quite different, is one of the motors of the Hegelian dialectic.[26] We shall hold that the formulation 'the generic multiple is the truth of the initial situation' is the motor of *a kind of dialectic*, a dialectical sequencing.

The most important feature to retain from this definition of the generic multiple is that it is constituted not only through a work of division, but also through a work of synthesis; not only does it proceed through negation – not that multiple, nor that one – but also through affirmation – some of that multiple, and some of the other. In the end, a generic procedure of fidelity is like some kind of inordinately fussy but endless shopping list in which the products to be bought have not even been made yet. But what guides this procedure of selection and synthesis, what decides whether or not a multiple is connected to the event? This is none other than the question of the consistency of a generic truth procedure; if the latter unfolds something indiscernible from the standpoint of established knowledge, then evidently no category of knowledge can guarantee its consistency – from the standpoint of established knowledge it is inconsistent. In *Being and Event*, Badiou claims that in each truth procedure an operator of fidelity emerges. As noted previously, this is an example of the philosophical desire for hetero-expulsion: philosophy expels its own problems into a different field or discursive practice: here Badiou has no general philosophical solution for the problem of the consistency of a generic procedure – apart from saying 'there is an operator of fidelity'. Of course he cannot possess such a solution, because otherwise philosophy would be in the position of unifying and discerning the multiplicity of indiscernible truth procedures.[27] Hence it is quite logical for him to argue that each truth-procedure creates its own form of consistency. His first example is the scientific truth procedure of set-theory ontology itself, for which the operator of fidelity is deduction. Our example shall be the work of Allan Kaprow, and also those members of the Fluxus movement such as Robert Filliou and Ben Vautier, who develop a fidelity to the event of Duchamp's ready-made in the field of art by conceiving it as a gesture rather than as a work of art. Within their enquiries, the operator of fidelity is thus the conception of the ready-made *as gesture*.[28] The global function of this operator of fidelity is to operate as a provisional name for an entire unknown art to come, indeed in the case of Kaprow, of a massive multiple that blurs the boundaries between art and life. This provisional name thus unites and synthesizes disparate and sometimes isolated artistic experiments as diverse expressions of the same unknown but consistent multiple.

In short, to assert the existence of a generic multiple is to assert that a procedure can hold together in the absence of objective and known guarantees. Whatever the obstacles, interruptions, losses of momentum and backlashes, irregardless of the geographical and historical separation of different enquiries, there is an underlying unknown and infinite consistency that remains to be unfolded, little by little. But how does this unfolding take place: in the absence of knowledge, how does one know whether one isn't simply replicating what has already been done in connection with the event?

Forcing, the work of the subject, supplementation and the old mole

In order to think the occurrence of a truth procedure at a local level, Badiou imports a second major concept from Paul Cohen's mathematics into philosophy: forcing. Forcing is an operation that allows knowledge to be gained about the new situation to come. The latter is called the 'generic extension' and it results from the initial situation being supplemented by its own generic subset as one of its elements. Badiou calls the operation of forcing the *law of the subject*. The law states that if one can show that a particular multiple of the situation entertains a knowable relationship with a statement about the situation to come, and if that particular multiple turns out to be connected to the event and hence an element of the generic multiple, then that statement will have been true of the situation to come (the generic extension). Forcing thus produces an anticipatory knowledge of the new situation, a knowledge that is *under condition* in that its truth is suspended from the chance of the enquiries. What Badiou provides with the operation of forcing is an account of the local and accumulative production of new knowledge: this is precisely what he was looking for in his early Althusserian research. Any theory of the production of knowledge has to furnish criteria for distinguishing knowledge from both error and tautology. In the case of the knowledge produced through forcing, Badiou stipulates that it is not just any statement that can be forced: some statements will not have a knowable relationship with any of the multiples of the situation, other statements will possess such a relationship with every multiple of the situation; only a particular kind of statement will possess a relationship with certain multiples and not others.

Forcing is not only a theory of knowledge for Badiou; it is also his theory of the subject. Rather than simply moving on from his work in *Théorie du sujet*, Badiou selectively incorporates and adapts parts of it under new names in *Being and Event*. Here it is the 'subjective process' that is reworked as 'forcing'. A subject in *Being and Event* is a fragment of a truth procedure; that is, a subject is a series of successful enquiries, a set of multiples connected to the name of the event. Thus in a political truth procedure a subject is not so much an agent as a series of meetings, tracts, protests and occupations of parliament. In an artistic truth procedure a subject could be a happening, a score or a sequence of poems. As a set of multiples connected to an event and encountered during the random sequence of enquiries, the subject falls outside the purview of ontology. Thus in Badiou's terms, ontology cannot think the *being* of the subject, but it can think its *operation*, which is forcing. There is no separation, however, between the subject's being as a set of multiples and forcing: a particular instance of forcing is what produces or unfolds that set of multiples. There is no room, therefore, for a part of the being of the subject that might be the source of forcing: in other words, there is no separate agent of change within the subject for Badiou. The subject is nothing but change as forcing. Take set-theory ontology itself as a truth procedure, as Badiou does in Meditation 20; the subject in this procedure is not Cantor the individual but Cantor as a series of unprecedented mathematical statements. The subject is not so much an agent behind the work of change, but the work of change itself.

What has changed in between *Théorie du sujet* and *Being and Event* is the role of destruction. In a brief exercise of self-critique – an exemplary Maoist practice – Badiou admits that previously he had mistaken the role of destruction in the process of creation. Here he argues that destruction only concerns the existence of established hierarchies and statements of value that are no longer accurate; it is never the case that a multiple itself is destroyed in the process of change. At a global level, that process, rather than being the division of a unity, as in his Maoist period, is now theorized as a slow supplementation of the initial situation with its indiscernible subset. The subset, as noted above, is added to the level of presentation as an element. This evidently disrupts the established structure of the situation and requires a complete – and gradual – reworking of that structure in order to accommodate the generic multiple as element. Moreover – and this is one of the key results of Cohen's mathematical construction of the generic multiple – inasmuch as the initial situation is infinite, so is the generic multiple. Strictly speaking, this entails that a generic truth procedure is forever unfinished – however far it has gone, it still remains to come. But this does not mean that an enquiry that takes place a long time after the initial event is in the same position as one near the beginning of the truth procedure. The enquiries into Greek tragedy named 'German idealism' in philosophy or even 'Nietzsche' are in quite a different position to the enquiry that consists of the Oedipus trilogy. What separates early and late enquiries is the emergence of what Badiou calls a *subject-idiom*, consisting of a plethora of new names whose reference is suspended from the existence of the new supplemented situation. This idiom serves to reinforce, instantiate and project the consistency of the truth procedure; at the level of structure it constitutes what Badiou terms *the counter-state*, a set of re-presentations or regroupings of multiples that have turned out to be connected to the event. The subject idiom and the counter-state are built up through the slow accumulation of the statements of forcing and together they provide a material solution to the question of the transmission of a truth procedure: there is no ascetic initiation for adepts of a truth procedure; all that exists is an accumulation of hypotheses about, for example, a new epic theatre. This conception of change as the gradual accumulation or *synthesis* of statements and names indicates just how far Badiou has travelled since his Maoist period, the period in which the dynamism of change and the avoidance of dead ends could only be guaranteed through perpetual division, a practice more than legible in the history of the left or Lacanian psychoanalysis in France. Not that Badiou embraces consensus; far from it, since a consensus always depends on established knowledge of the situation. A generic procedure of fidelity remains a work of division, but it also develops through new unprecedented syntheses. It is in this model of slow relentless supplementation of a situation that we find again that tendency, that voice in Badiou's thought of change that is the old mole. What remains to be seen is whether it is the old mole, the owl or the eagle that prevails in the *Being and Event* theory of change.

The problem of voluntarism

One of the more recurrent critiques aimed at Badiou's theory of change, as mentioned above, is voluntarism. One variation on this objection begins by asking whether a truth procedure is subject to any constraints and concludes that in the absence of moral criteria there is nothing that separates a political truth procedure from the worst politics in history, in particular National Socialism and Stalinism. Badiou's conception amounts to thinking political practice as the sheer expression of a subjective will. Moreover, from an external viewpoint, in the absence of moral criteria Badiou's philosophy celebrates change for the sake of change. This objection is useful for our interpretation since it is evident that Badiou is quite aware of it and shapes his theory in response. It also condenses many of the premises of an approach to politics via morality, which is precisely what he sets out to critique in his *Ethics*.

Badiou's sensitivity to this kind of objection can be measured to some degree by the number of constraints that are actually built into his theory of change: five. First, a generic truth procedure is initiated by a true rather than a mythic event, and a true event is one that occurs within an evental site. This is what allows Badiou to disqualify the 'revolution' of National Socialism from being an event: rather than occurring in an opaque excluded area of the political situation, this so-called revolution addressed an already constituted multiple that was both present and re-presented within the situation – the German people.[29] Such a disqualification, by the way, indicates why criteria other than the actual occurrence of an event are required to identify evental sites. The second constraint concerns the actual shape of the fidelity – Badiou discerns three different types of fidelity: a *dogmatic* fidelity which claims that all multiples of the situation are connected to the event, regardless of their nature; a *spontaneist* fidelity that asserts that only the multiples of the evental site itself are connected to the event, asserting a kind of exclusive purity of original proximity to the event and thus no possibility of transmission (BE, 237). A *generic* fidelity, however, is one that starts out from the premise of ignorance as to which multiples are actually connected to the event, and continues via the wager that some multiples will turn out to be connected. This leads us to the third constraint on a truth procedure, which is quite simply that at a local level it may turn out that certain multiples are not connected to the event. For instance, if the operator of fidelity in the generic truth procedure called modernist theatre is the definition of theatre as a 'collective creative act', as Meyerhold declares, then Jerzy Grotowski's slow removal of the audience from theatrical experience turns out, at its limit, not to belong to the truth procedure of modernist theatre. The reason is that its collective – that of the troupe of actors – exists previous to and independently of any particular performance. Meyerhold's operator of fidelity, however, prescribes the irruption, within any particular performance, of a temporary but unique collective. The critic could return that the voluntarism thus lies in the choice of the operator of fidelity, but such an operator is not so much chosen once and for all but replicated and transmitted by many subjects. It takes more than one enquiry to make a fidelity generic. The fourth constraint concerns the effects of forcing. Badiou is at pains to emphasize that a statement may well disqualify certain terms of the ancient situation from their hitherto privileged positions: for instance, theatrical space no longer has to be dominated by the multiple that we call the 'fourth wall'. However, the experimentation with alternative conceptions of theatrical space and the recurrent attempts to bring the audience and performers together do not necessarily entail the complete suppression of the use of the fourth wall. Badiou terms this disqualification yet maintenance of a multiple *saving the singular* (BE, 406–7). Finally, in his *Ethics*, Badiou adds the fifth constraint on the direction of a truth procedure. He claims that in each of the four domains of truth – love, art, politics and science – there exists a term that is subtracted from the operations of any truth procedure, the *unnameable*.[30] In the field of politics it is the social bond; in the field of love it is sexual enjoyment itself. If a generic truth procedure attempts to rename and remake this term, the result is an evil that Badiou names disaster.[31] The existence of these five constraints may or may not convince our normative opponent: the meta-constraint, of course, on

Badiou's responses to such concerns is that he must devise immanent structural constraints on the genericity of a truth-procedure. Badiou's commitment to an infinity of situations and to the indiscernibility of change prevents him from constructing a transcendental morality or socially grounded model of ideal political action.

The accusation of voluntarism, however, raises another question, which is that of the conceptualization of the will, especially given that Badiou turns to Rousseau's concept of the general will to provide a philosophical exegesis of the generic multiple in politics. Any investigation of the emergence of a will in Badiou's concept of generic truth procedures must first pass via Nietzsche's critique and use of the notion of will. The target of Nietzsche's critique of the psychological notion of free will is its presupposition of a clear separation between the doer and the deed and its simplification of complex unknown chains of organic causality into a simple cause – the free agent or will – and the effect – the intended action. The transposition of this critique into Badiou's conception of change would focus on the supposition of a self-identical unified agent of change. It is clear that Badiou's concept of the subject precludes any such unified entity that is not part of the change itself; however, what does occur in the truth procedure is the supposition of *something being at work* through its unfolding. This is precisely what Nietzsche argues that we should posit faced with the unknown chains of causality that link mental events to activities and that are at work through human consciousness: 'Man is not only a single individual but one particular line in the total organic world.'[32] The overcoming of man, for Nietzsche, takes place initially through the recognition that 'consciousness' and 'purposes' are mere epiphenomena through which something else – ultimately the will to power – is at work. In the context of Badiou's truth procedures, the wager of the existence of unknown consistency amounts to the positing of a *hypokeimenon* or substrate, a term that Lacan picks up to think the unconscious with regard to clinical symptoms. However, there is a difference between presuming that a unified entity is the cause of all of one's actions, and wagering that there is something that lies beneath which remains to be discovered and unfolded. The difference between the positing of a *hypokeimenon* in a generic procedure and Nietzsche's 'line in the total organic world' or Aristotle's pure matter as substrate is that the generic multiple will prove accessible to knowledge through forcing. Nevertheless, what is common to Nietzsche and Badiou is the heuristic moment of thought which recognizes an action not as a construction but as an expression of something lying beneath; indeed Badiou says within a truth procedure 'there is *a law of the not-known*.[33] That is, the identification of multiples connected to the event is at the same time recognition of their status as metonymies of something much larger – the generic multiple.

The emergence of such a thinking of expression has a consequence at the level of ontology. Badiou does not simply critique and dismiss a Nietzschean – or even Deleuzean – ontology of expression as a vitalist restoration of a unity of being that falls short of the injunction to think infinite multiplicity; rather, like Hegel with his placement of rival philosophies as necessary moments in the unfolding of the Absolute, Badiou places an ontology of expression as a transitory but necessary heuristic within the pragmatics of change.[34]

Thus Badiou does not develop a voluntarist theory of change, but from within a procedure of change it is necessary to posit the as yet unknown existence of something like a higher or deeper will – that can and will surface.

The permanency of the state, right-Badiousianism and the owl

But why would one trust a higher or deeper will? I owe this question, admirable in its concision, to Carlos Frade: his counter to my injunction to pay heed to movements in the sub-basements of Europe as heralds of political change – 'why trust something that comes from below?'[35] Such questions must be admitted as soon as Badiou abandons Marxism as political economy – in his Maoist period – and then abandons Marxism as a theory of revolution – in his current period. That is, if Badiou has no account of alienation or exploitation, if he has no account of the structural exclusion of the proletariat from politics, then how can he qualify a truth procedure as good? Or rather, why is there an imperative running through his philosophy to throw oneself out of one's outside, to cite Celan? There is certainly a rhetoric of immortality at work in his texts; a celebration of the human animal's occasional participation in a subject as part of an eternal truth procedure: does Badiou share the desire of Thetis? Why should one choose to become Achilles? The short answer is that there are no ethical criteria external to a truth procedure: the good is precisely what is remade and renamed in a generic practice. When Badiou does elaborate an *ethic of truths* in response to this kind of question, it is a formal ethics which stipulates the conditions that allow a human animal to continue participating in a truth procedure, rather than qualifying the content of that procedure. One doesn't 'trust' a truth procedure, one is taken up by it if – and only if – one recognizes that the initial event does concern the situation; if one decides that it makes sense for guest-workers to demand political rights, then one is engaged in the consequent political procedure.

A similar objection can be raised from a Marxist angle: once Badiou's theory of change removes all traces of the revolutionary dialectic, how can one be assured that a political procedure will lead to communism and the withering away of the state? We saw in *Théorie du sujet* that the unfinished task of Maoism – and the short-lived promise of the Chinese Cultural Revolution – was precisely to think of the transition to communism as the withering away of the state and the disappearance of class. Badiou examines this question from the standpoint of the critique and destruction of the party, which is none other than the question of periodization. Periodization occurs through division; thus there is no 'final victory' in the Maoist conception of the dialectic, but a permanent cycle of historical sequences of victory and defeat. In this conception, rather than as a form of utopia, communism would be identified as this very process of division, this continual destruction and remaking of state structures.

But then what happens in *Being and Event*? How does the thinker of permanent division become the thinker of the ubiquity of the state in all situations? Does Badiou give up the idea of the withering away of the state in *Being and Event*? On my first reading of *Being and Event*, as a PhD student raised on Marxist and post-structuralist attempts to think of community without the state, I was disappointed by what I saw as its flatly anti-utopian side – despite the occurrence of a generic procedure, the state survives as a structuring principle in the new situation. And the disappointment in this seeming apology for a permanence of injustice was all the more keenly felt precisely because I had given up on various post-structuralisms for the idealism and utopianism of their archi-political stance.[36] However, like most PhD students, I was misguided and my first reading was clouded by shades of Jean-Luc Nancy and Maurice Blanchot. The state, for Badiou, is an ontological concept and is not equivalent to the political state. It designates a second structuring principle, after the initial count-for-one, that gathers together all possible regroupings of multiples presented in the situation. Recognizing the ubiquity of this structuring principle is thus not the same as embracing the permanence of injustice. Indeed ubiquity is not the same as permanence: the state of a new supplemented situation is not the same state as that of the initial situation – this is precisely why it is called the *counter-state* while it is being constructed. What counts as art for curators and art critics now is not the same as what counted as art for the organizers of the 1916 Salon in New York; those who originally rejected R. Mutt's entry.

So a sop can be thrown to my youthful idealism – like a honey-soaked rag down the throat of Cerberus – Badiou does not embrace perpetual structures of exclusion that only gain longevity through their occasional assimilation of events. But here again a great risk arises, the risk of *Right-Badiousianism*. If a truth procedure simply replaces one state with another state, one ordering mechanism with another such mechanism, then all states can be understood as being originally counter-states. All established political institutions could be analysed and defended as extended faithful enquiries into the consequences of an original event. In the hands of these exegetes, Badiou's philosophy would thus end up by producing an apology for modern parliamentary democracies. Badiou would then, despite himself, join the ranks of his preferred enemies, the ex-Maoist apostate *nouveaux philosophes*. A perilous risk indeed! Something must be done.

The right Badiousian begins his argument by declaring: 'there are no external criteria to judge the desirability of a generic procedure, generic procedures simply occur, people are either taken up by them or not; ordering mechanisms simply replace one another over time'. Our first step in warding off this peril is thus to identify the beast behind such a declaration: with such a long distance view of history, recalling the sequence of dialectical periodizations of structure in *Théorie du sujet*, it can be none other than the owl. The virtue of the owl lies in its distance from the hurly burly of actual historical events; this distance is supposed to lend it the lofty neutrality or indifference of objectivity. But if the owl's declarations end in an apology for all established institutions as instances of slow-moving change, then its objectivity is confined to a very few objects; those that are well anchored in the present. The owl emerges at its purest in theories of the cyclical birth and death of civilizations such as those of Arnold Toynbee and Oswald Spengler. The common characteristic of such *social cycle* theories is that they naturalize change – often explicitly with recourse to climate change models to explain long-term change in human settlement patterns. It is the foundational reference to nature that provides the key for a diagnosis of the owl: the owl depends on an identification of change with genesis. In the exegesis of *Being and Event*, the owl advances a genetic interpretation of the count-for-one and claims that all situations are generated through generic truth procedures. This is evidently an unorthodox reading and many passages from the text can be marshalled against it, first among which would be the distinction between natural and historical situations.

But the owl cannot be silenced so easily; it originates in Badiou's early work, precisely in his reconstruction of Althusser's problematic of the emergence of new knowledge. Recall the argument of Chapter 1: in his theory of change Althusser fuses the questions of unity, order and change such that change is identified with the genesis of the whole. In so doing he reproduces the Aristotelian productivist model of change and inherits its problems, first amongst which is that unless one admits the religious model of *creation ex nihilo*, one must posit that change is the change of something and thus there is something that lies beneath and remains the same throughout change – the *hypokeimenon* again! In so far as the Aristotelian holds that all beings are unified and self-identical, the *hypokeimenon* is problematic because it is both supposed to remain the same, as the bearer of change, and yet at the same time *change* in so far as its form must be different once the change is complete. The modern solution to this problem is the one Badiou adopts in his reconstruction of Althusser: one posits a structure composed of various elements and then one conceives change as the re-combination and shuffling of such elements. But this solution will not satisfy the later Badiou: the sign of a global transformation is the emergence of a new situation, not the reorganization of an already existing situation. If the Aristotelian matrix were exhaustive for the philosophy of change, Badiou would then have to adopt a variation of the *creation ex nihilo* model of change, whereas in fact he condemns such models under the name of speculative leftism for their dreams of absolute beginning – models that we condemn, of course, as the fantasy of the eagle. But there are other paths in philosophy than those marked by Aristotle, and so Badiou thinks change as the supplementation of a situation: something remains the same – the elements of the initial multiple – but something is changed – the structure of that multiple, in as much as its count-for-one is forced to accommodate a new element, the generic multiple. Change is not thought of as the production of a situation but as the extension, expansion and supplementation of a situation: here we recognize the voice of the old mole.

The risk of Right Badiousianism can thus be diagnosed as the risk of the voice of the owl dominating the theory of change. The best defence against such an interpretation is to mobilize another of the voices: the old mole. Ultimately the question is whether or not these voices balance each other out within Badiou's philosophy.

The eagle, the owl and the old mole

The eagle, despite appearances, is also an autochthonous voice in Badiou. Badiou criticizes Nietzsche for having an absolutist model of change, for proclaiming his desire to 'break the history of the world in two'; and yet what does an event do, in its anomalous irruption, but cause a situation to be slowly divided in two: into those multiples connected to the event, and those non-connected. The intervention itself, as I argue above, in its miraculous conversion of undecidability into decision and impossibility into possibility, gives rise to a punctual model of change. The separation between established knowledge and the 'truth' of the generic procedure, if taken as absolute, creates a pure body of change and subsequently gives rise to a confusion of fidelity with dogmatic belief. This is precisely the critique that Slavoj Žižek and Peter Osborne level at Badiou.[37]

Granted these are each identifiable and comprehensible risks in the interpretation of Badiou, but what holds them all together in this absurd figure of the eagle? What is the eagle's model of change? Its first defining characteristic is that it admits the existence of an identifiable unique point at the outset of the change. The second characteristic is that this point is understood, after Aristotle, as an efficient cause, as a self-identical agent responsible for the entirety of the effectuation of the change. Unlike Aristotle, however, this point is also conceived as immediately revealing or containing the entirety of the change: the change is prepared, foreshadowed, heralded; the initial punctuation is pregnant with its future. In the field of art, this model of change can be found in the invocation of inspiration as *source* for the work of art. In the field of religion, this model can be found in the invocation of the coming of the messiah as sufficient for the transformation of earthly life. In Aristotelian terms this model depends on a conflation of the efficient and the formal cause. In short, in the eyes of the eagle, the opening up of the initial point of change is enough to realize an immediate subjectivization of the whole of its context. The eagle short-circuits the figure of the One – the miraculous point – with the figure of the Totality – the immediately transfigured situation. This short-circuit produces a model of change not only as spectacle – the whole of the change can be surveyed – but also as felt presence and experience: if the whole situation is subjectivized then conversely the change may be circumscribed by one subject alone, precisely as *passion*.

Badiou is well aware of the presence of the eagle in his thought of change as an internal temptation and risk. His name for this tendency is

Nietzsche – and his defences are multiple. There is no angelic herald of the event – such as the madman or Zarathustra arriving in the town square – since the existence of an evental site is merely a necessary but non-sufficient condition for the occurrence of an event. Moreover, there is no hero of the event in that the intervention is actually never secure: the undecidability of the event continually re-emerges and its belonging must be decided anew in each enquiry. Finally, against speculative left-ism, change occurs not through creation but through slow supplementation. Being – Badiou declares – does not commence (BE, 210–11).

If the eagle is a model of change that Badiou rejects why is his theory of change not completely free of it? Why does it emerge as a voice in his work? In a materialist theory of change, as Badiou realizes in his early work on Althusser, the starting point of change must be both immanent and locatable: hence the necessity for an initial point. Once change is understood as subjectivization, as Badiou realizes in *Théorie du sujet*, then its very impetus must reside in the *promise* of total subjectivization of the situation. When Badiou characterizes what he took from Sartre, he writes: 'the entire world, in its given order, is of no interest except if it is taken up and reworked according to the subjective prescription of a project whose extension measures up to it.'[38] In other words, each finite enquiry must orientate itself as part of an infinite change. Hence, the eagle, in part, is necessary.

But let us be English – to Nietzsche's disgust – and insist upon the parallel necessity of the slow pragmatic process of supplementation; that is, on the role of the old mole. If the promise of the subjectivization of everything is necessary as a heuristic declaration within a generic procedure, it nevertheless does not amount to an assertion of the infinity of that procedure. An infinite multiple is not a totality; especially given the undoing of the classic part–whole relationship through the axiom of the powerset. Indeed, strictly speaking, from an external point of view – which Badiou names that of the *ontologist* – the infinity of the generic set cannot be totalized by a unifying name from within its situation. From the ontologist's standpoint, the infinity of the truth procedure is guaranteed by the infinity of the initial situation, but what of the standpoint of the *inhabitant* of the situation? From the perspective of the enquiries, how can their finitude make up an infinite procedure? We know from Badiou's own exegesis of the axiom of infinity that an endless succession of finite ordinal sets is not sufficient to constitute an infinite set: one must declare the existence of an infinite set within which that succession unfolds. What is the equivalent to such a declaration within a truth procedure? How is it possible for a finite enquiry to orientate itself as part of an infinite process? Note that this is none other than the question of the encounter of the infinite with the finite: a question religion answers with each of its scenes of immortal–mortal interaction, in prophecy, divine dreams, incarnation or even the ritual of the eucharist. A materialist answer to this question would require a theory of revolutionary speech acts, of particular instances of forcing which as performatives have the effect of repositioning an enquiry within an infinite horizon. In the political realm this is what Kant called the question of revolutionary enthusiasm. In general, it is the question of transmission. At present, it is *the* question of critical philosophy.

If both the old mole and the eagle have roles to play in Badiou's theory of change, how do they interact? The event – the eagle's initiation of change – consists of the elements of the evental site plus its own name. The evental site, as I argue above, consists of an encounter between heterogeneous situations. Forcing – the work of the old mole – consists in amassing those multiples that are connected to the event. Thus forcing can be understood as the slow expansion of the evental site; it extends and exacerbates the original point of opacity at which the event occurred. In its continual assertion that this opaque enlarged multiple belongs to the situation, forcing breaks with the established distribution of the situation's parts. In doing so, the enquiries create new parts or neighbourhoods with as yet unknown boundaries. For this reason the enquiries practise what can be called *a logic of incompletion*. This incompletion affects not only the original boundaries of the evental site and the established partition of the situation, but finally the very boundaries of the situation itself. For this reason – and Badiou himself does not draw such extreme conclusions – the very existence and activity of generic truth procedures within the domains of art, politics, science and love could lead, through infinite expansion of evental sites, to *either* the complete indetermination of those domains *or* their renaming.[39] Badiou has sat philosophy on a volcano.

Before its top blows, and all our categories become obsolete, note that the old mole is thus the dialectization of the eagle. But then what can we make of the owl? Must the seat of Right Badiousianism be struck from his philosophy or does it also have its own role to play?

The virtue of the owl is that it advances a neutral description of change – and thus prevents any imposition of a transcendental schema of the good, since the domains of change are irreversibly disparate in their multiplicity. In this instance the owl insists on the rights of the generic, on the overall result of the dialectic of the old mole and the eagle: a new unprecedented situation. On the other hand, the owl also asserts that whether or not change occurs in one particular situation, change has and will occur somewhere. It thus has the virtue of orientating our research towards events that have either already happened, or are happening in situations further afield than our habitual haunts. As such the owl draws a line from the work of the old mole and the eagle to the renovation of philosophy itself: the owl flies out of the volcano.

To finish this exegesis of Badiou's conception of change on a strictly hyperbolic note, I shall advance one last interpretative claim. The concept of a generic truth procedure realizes a fusion of Aristotle's categories of *praxis* (action) and *poiesis* (production) and *theoria* (speculation). In doing so it provides yet one more philosophical answer to philosophy's oldest question: 'what is the good life?'

What takes place in an enquiry, from the point of view of an enquiry, is both the actualization of a potential form hidden in the matter of the situation – like Aristotle's production. At the same time, of course, the inhabitant of a truth procedure must also conceive of their activity as the invention of a new form, in so far as it is still unclear just how the form belongs to the situation, how it is placed regionally, what order it invokes and how it connects to the global. In turn, inasmuch as a truth procedure entails the transformation of humans into subjects it can be conceived as a form of *praxis*: the chief characteristic of *praxis* for Aristotle was its effectuation of a change in the situation of its subject. Speculation or theory for Aristotle is knowledge of the principles of beings, and in so far as forcing produces knowledge of new multiples speculation is indeed part of a generic procedure. Finally, if the work of enquiries takes place as both effortful construction and as the revelation of something already at work, then one has a fusion of freedom and necessity. Such is the good life for philosophy.

Method

Two objections: verification and redundancy

Between *Théorie du sujet* and *L'être et l'événement* there is a transformation of Badiou's philosophy: the first places itself as a moment within the revolutionary dialectic of knowledge, the second places itself squarely within the tradition of French and German philosophy. The interrupted enquiries into heteroclite sources, the implicit shifts in vocabulary, the revisions of provisional theses have all disappeared: in their place a magisterial discourse which sets out its arguments in a gradual and accumulative manner; *Being and Event* unfolds a systematic philosophy complete with axioms, doctrines and its own mechanism of perpetual renovation – the definition of philosophy as the construction of a coherent conceptual space for contemporary truth procedures, or conditions, in the domains of art, politics, science and love. In turn, there has been a change in how Badiou's philosophy contextualizes itself: from polemics aimed at leftist and rightist deviations of the revolutionary dialectic, to multiple polemics directed against the linguistic turn in philosophy (baptized *idealinguistery*), hermeneutics, philosophies of finitude (and their declarations of the end of philosophy), contemporary sophistry, anti-philosophy (Nietzsche, Wittgenstein, Lacan) and finally, in a massive widening of the stage of Badiou's philosophy, democratic materialism, the ideology of our times which proclaims 'there are only bodies and languages'.

The ground of all of these polemics is Badiou's identification of mathematics with ontology. There are two main charges laid against this identification in the commentary around Badiou's philosophy. The first is that set-theory ontology is a castle built in the air with no relation to reality: the world has been lost. The second objection is that the set theory itself is redundant; Badiou's 'metaontology' is nothing but a meticulous recoding of established philosophical concepts – such as interpretation – in mathematical form.[40] Any reader of Badiou can find resources to dismiss these objections: the first is based on a model of truth as adequation and the Cartesian supposition that discourses can be founded; the second simply ignores the difference between mathematical ideas and philosophical concepts. However, such objections do have the virtue of awakening us from any dogmatic slumber: Badiou's development of a set-theory ontology raises as many questions as it resolves. The simplest of these questions is what does one do with a set-theory ontology? Should one carry out ontological analyses of particular situations to determine their structure of multiplicity, or set? And if so, according to which protocols of analysis? Badiou's response to a question of this type was quite emphatic:

> We have a concrete situation. We can think the ontological structure of that situation. So we can think about infinite multiplicity, something about the natural multiplicity . . . the historical character of the situation . . . the eventual site and so on. There is an ontological schema of the situation. With this schema we can understand the situation.[41]

But how exactly can these structures be thought if, as Badiou admits in his article 'One, Multiple, Multiplicities', there is no procedure of verification available to determine the adequation of the ontological analysis to its concrete situation?[42] To answer this question first we must situate it: when, according to Badiou's philosophy, does one speak of a situation being an infinite multiple or possessing an evental multiple; when does one do, not ontology, but *metaontology* for Badiou?

The answer is quite simply within the enquiries of a particular generic truth procedure: that is when decisions are made on existence, and a situation is schematized in a pragmatic and heuristic manner. Indeed in 'One, Multiple, Multiplicities' he continues by saying 'the theory of the multiple . . . can only serve as a regulative ideal for prescriptions'. Of course, this does not mean that all militants analyse what is to be done in terms of 'evental sites' and 'infinite multiplicity'; but their declarations and prescriptions do take the form of isolating points of exception and expanding the horizons of possibility. Metaontology would not be invented – that happens in philosophy – but would take place as particular kinds of speech act that advance generic truth procedures. Moreover, Badiou clearly states in the interview in *Infinite Thought* that it is only in the occurrence of disaster and dysfunction that the true structure of a situation – its metaontological schema – can be traced: as noted above, this is his epistemological variation on the thesis of the primacy of practice.[43] The 'verification', therefore, of these kinds of schema, is strictly speaking none other than the production of new objects of knowledge, or new practices, within the enquiries of generic truth procedures.

The second objection claims that the thesis of the identity of ontology and mathematics does no philosophical work because the set theory is redundant; all it does is re-transcribe established concepts. It would be nice to know exactly which well-established philosophical concept is re-transcribed by Paul Cohen's operation of forcing. But let's not squabble: the more interesting question is what exactly does this thesis do. We know that the doctrine of conditions states that philosophy develops its concepts under the condition of contemporary truth procedures whose results it captures in concepts. In doing so philosophy is constrained to construct a space of compossibility for these concepts. However, philosophy retains some sovereignty in deciding which contemporary truth procedures to name and conceptualize. Once it does name a certain generic truth procedure – such as set theory – there are ineluctable consequences: the first is that philosophy's established concepts will be displaced and its habitual arguments will be interrupted. For example, Badiou, the thinker of the withering away of the state, is forced to admit the ubiquity of the state as an ontological structure. Second example: the axiom of foundation clearly destabilizes Badiou's philosophical doctrine of the regionalization of being into natural and historical situations. Subsequently Badiou is forced to rework his concept of evental-site as he admits in *Logiques des mondes*. The second major consequence of conditioning is possible obsolescence: mathematical results may be surpassed by new results, a particular conception of justice may be rendered obsolete – in turn the philosophy conditioned by those mathematical results and political conceptions will no longer be contemporary.[44] This foundation of philosophy on the contingency of truth procedures is a direct transcription of the Maoist primacy of practice thesis: it is also precisely how Badiou undermines the traditional self-sufficiency of philosophy.

But what are the particular consequences of naming set theory 'ontology' and conceptualizing its results? It so happens that the development of set-theory ontology and category-theory phenomenology provide us with the most radical and asymmetrical examples of conditioning to be found in Badiou's work. Philosophy is not only interrupted and placed under the shadow of future changes, but it has had entire areas of its traditional competency taken away from it. If a symmetrical procedure happened with aesthetics via artistic generic procedures, moral philosophy via amorous procedures, and political philosophy via political procedures, one could well ask what would remain of philosophy? But at the same time as ontology is handed over to mathematics, philosophy develops a new discourse called 'metaontology', and in relation to particular artistic procedures it no longer offers definitions of beauty but develops a new discourse called 'inaesthetics'. Thus philosophy does not risk extinction through conditioning but rather transformation. From this standpoint, what then is to be done with Badiou's metaontology? The general prescription of Badiou's philosophy is not to engage in pure exegesis but always to develop one's arguments on the basis of a conditioning of philosophy: such a conditioning could be mathematical and lead to a supplement or a reworking of Badiou's metaontology. Consequently it is only through further philosophical experiences of conditioning that the initial thesis 'mathematics is ontology' can be criticized or supported. In the end, the justification for this thesis can be none other than its consequences: the ensemble of philosophical propositions that it gives rise to, the whole of *Being and Event* and then the further construction of *Logiques des mondes*.

Philosophy and its conditions

Two features mark Badiou's doctrine of conditions as radically different to his Maoist placement of philosophy as part of the revolutionary dialectic of knowledge. The first is the stipulation that philosophy be separated from its conditions under pain of what Badiou terms 'disaster'. Whenever philosophy believes itself capable of identifying the essence of politics, or science, or art, or love, it attempts a *fusion* with one of its conditions. In doing so it develops a normative model of politics or science, etc. and thus disqualifies any possible novelty emerging within that field. The consequences are no less serious for philosophy in that its prospects rise and fall with the particular instance of politics or science that has been identified as the ideal and the norm. In retrospect, Badiou diagnoses Althusser's work as a fusion of philosophy with politics. The second stipulation – a painful admission for Badiou – is that if a generic procedure unfolds the truth of its situation, philosophy itself does not unfold or declare truths. Philosophy is placed in a secondary position, that of identifying, conceptualizing and renaming the truth that emerges within a particular generic procedure. Philosophy, moreover, must guard that its names are separate to the names and idiom of a particular truth procedure.[45]

It is only when one becomes familiar with Badiou's Maoist work that one is really struck by the piety of this doctrine of conditions with its careful stipulations of separation and its restrictions on philosophy's ambition to name worlds. This piety has a source: though I cannot justify my suspicions here, I hold that the source is Badiou's encounter with the work of Philippe Lacoue-Labarthe and Jean-Luc Nancy. While Badiou stages his immunity to their thought via an open attack in his *Manifesto* on philosophies of finitude and the theme of the end of philosophy, in the wings his own philosophy was gradually ceding to the temptation of admitting its own finitude, its own 'ethical' limitation. Any such limitation, in my eyes, is incoherent with the more radical drives of Badiou's philosophy. Take the idea of the active *subtraction* of a generic truth procedure from the established categories of the state of its situation. Those categories include names for the totality of the situation and for its boundaries. If a truth procedure is actually generic, it undoes every category of the state including those that fix the boundaries and identity of the initial situation. We know that at an ontological level a truth procedure changes the very structure of its situation through adding the generic multiple at the level of presentation: this is termed the 'generic extension'. How could a generic procedure – infinite in its extension – not affect the supposed boundary between its own situation and that of philosophy? Philosophy, in Badiou's own terms, is a presented multiplicity just like mathematics: that philosophy be capable of ceding part of its territory to mathematics is a sign of the latter's infection of philosophy. That philosophy be conducted, inside and outside universities, in the form of the lecture, and that its texts continually strive to encompass their own context are signs that philosophy has been infected by theatre, since the Greeks. Once one admits the existence of generic multiples, instantiates their dynamism as procedures, and stipulates their strictly infinite extension, one cannot simply erect an impervious boundary between one's discipline and their activity. To think a generic truth procedure is to embark upon what I call an *explosive genealogy* wherein all established philosophical categories are subject to a gradual but inexorable decomposition. Thus the thesis 'philosophy does not produce truths' must be reassigned: it is only from a viewpoint that believes itself to be philosophical that one cannot declare the 'truth' of an art such as theatre by, for example, defining tragedy. Philosophy cannot encompass its conditions. But the inverse is not true. From the standpoint of a condition, which may or may not have infected philosophy, the truth of a generic procedure could quite easily *pass through* part of a philosophical text. Truth procedures actively *incomplete* philosophy. Hence when philosophy names generic procedures among its external conditions, at the same time it could well be unknowingly naming part of itself. The doctrine of conditions thus leads to a transformation of philosophy by revealing how it has already been and is being and will have been transformed by those truth procedures that are at work within.

Method in his Maoism: dialectical braiding versus modelling

Conditioning is the global name for Badiou's method in the period of *Being and Event*. In hindsight it would also appear to be his method in the Maoist period since *Théorie du sujet* develops its concepts through enquiries into political sequences, poems, psychoanalysis and fragments of mathematics. There is certainly a resemblance but on the other hand we know that *Peut-on penser la politique?* enshrined the abandon of an explicitly Marxist vocabulary. Such an act has to have had an effect on the level of Badiou's method. To start this enquiry we need to characterize his method in *Théorie du sujet*. Throughout that work, as shown in detail in the previous chapter, Badiou turns to disparate sources,

identifies concepts and then divides them: among materialist epistemologies Badiou identifies and divides four concepts of truth; in mathematics he identifies and divides algebra and topology and within
psychoanalysis, Badiou identifies divides two concepts of the real (TS,
139, 246, 243–4). He also, in a Hegelian turn, occasionally shows how
two apparently opposed tendencies – anarchism and structuralism –
actually form a unified couple (TC, 65). More consistently, when he
identifies and divides concepts, he devalues certain concepts such as
truth as adequation, or the real as excluded cause. However, he does not
dismiss them as errors or accidents of thought but incorporates them as
necessary moments of the movement of thought: he operates a synthesis. Division and synthesis from diverse sources: Badiou's method in
Theorie du sujet is thus dialectical; he weaves a dialectical braid, with the
occasional loose thread. Even at the level of his masters he engages in a
game of division and synthesis: dividing Hegel by synthesizing him with
Lacan and playing Mao against both.

But what happens at the local level of one of the enquiries in *Théorie
du sujet*: how, for example, does Badiou read Mallarmé's sonnet and
extract a concept of the real as vanishing cause of the structural dialectic? Philosophers, as some literary critics will tell you, are appallingly
bad readers of poetry. They impose their clunky ponderous conceptual
schemes and crush the semantic complexity and historical specificity of
the literary text. Philosophers, we are told, use literature as a mere
illustration of a theory.[46] Is Badiou guilty of such a crime? In *Théorie du
sujet* there is no reading as close and detailed as that of Mallarmé's
sonnet, but the result of that reading is to declare that the poem stages
the structural dialectic itself. Badiou is most decidedly guilty! Not so fast.
Whenever a philosophical exchange is reduced to a courtroom setting
with accusations and pleas something is lost. And what falls out here is
that Badiou's reading of Mallarmé actually complicates his conception
of the structural dialectic by adding the Mallarméan figure of chance
producing the idea. 'Even worse!' the literary critic howls, 'imposition
and appropriation!' But what actually happens in Badiou's reading is far
stranger than the banalities of imposition and appropriation that constitute the everyday goings-on of all intellectual disciplines, including literary criticism.

Badiou, at the beginning of his interpretation, states that Mallarmé's
sea and air are a metaphor for the *splace* of the dialectic (TS, 94). In turn,
the foam is the metaphor of the offsite (TS, 95). The foam is the trace of
either a shipwreck or of a mermaid's dive, both metaphors of the causality of lack. Badiou's reading thus finds the same vanishing cause of

structure in this sonnet as he did in the Greek atomists. But then, in a second moment, Badiou claims that the sonnet does not simply consist of a series of metaphors for the structural dialectic, it does not simply represent the disappearance of an event (the siren's plunge, the shipwreck); it is part of the workings of the structural dialectic, it is the drama of a disappearing event. Moreover that event is the structural dialectic itself: 'The poem is no longer metaphor of the categories of the dialectic. It is their concept. The reality of the categories is at work to move the poetic thing . . . What the poem says, it does' (TS, 99). Badiou thus attributes self-reflexivity to the poem: what it says is a reflection of what it actually does, which is to stage the vanishing of the concept of the structural dialectic under the surface of the sea. This will not be the first time that Badiou reads a poem as self-reflexive – see his reading of Paul Valéry's 'Le cimetière marin' in *Logiques des mondes* – and as we shall see, self-reflexivity proves a very important structure in his thinking, not the least because it provides the essence, he claims, of all Marxist texts: both prescription and partial fulfilment of that prescription (TS, 99–100). But our poorly outlined conceptual personage of the literary critic is still upset: whether one attributes self-reflexivity or not one is still asserting that a literary text, a weave of signifiers, can be reduced to one transcendental signified which is 'the structural dialectic'. In Badiou's defence, he is only following Mallarmé's own lead; the first title of 'Ses purs ongles très hauts . . .' was 'sonnet allégorique de lui-même' (TS, 119). What is interesting, though, is what actually goes on in the substitution of one signifier (philosophical) for others (poetical). When Badiou lays out the sequence of metaphors he produces the following diagram (M_o for metaphor):

offsite	$\rightarrow$	writing	$\rightarrow$	foam
splace	M_o	blank	M_o	nude

What this diagram suggests is that 'offsite' is a metaphor for Mallarmé's own 'writing' which in turn is a metaphor for the sonnet's 'foam'. If Badiou were placing his philosophical signifiers as the signified of the poem it would be the other way around. Rather, what is at stake here is an attempt to prolong and extend the metaphorical substitutions already at work in Mallarmé's oeuvre by adding his own signifiers as further metaphors. Mallarmé's signifiers are thus placed as the signified of Badiou's theory. For this reason one can say that Badiou's method of reading is in a very strict, rather than a derogatory sense, metaphorical.

This is an odd method indeed but it has an antecedent in Badiou's work. In *Le concept de modèle*, as outlined in Chapter 1, Badiou explains a mathematical operation which constructs a syntax using a series of specific marks and rules for their combination resulting in a set of axioms. Subsequently, values from a particular semantic domain are assigned to each of the axioms or theorems of the syntax. If the axioms can be shown to be consistent with each other once assigned these semantic values, and if the various theorems can still be derived then it is said that a *model* has been produced of the original syntax, or theory. It is precisely such an operation which is at work in Badiou's reading of Mallarmé's sonnet: semantic values, such as 'foam' or 'siren', are assigned to the syntax of the structural dialectic, and then the re-evaluated dialectic is tested for its completion within the semantic field of the sonnet. If all of its operations – and Badiou reconstructs each of his categories, strong and weak difference, the vanishing cause, etc. – are restored within the sonnet then the reading of the sonnet is a model for the theory.

But what is the point of this method? In Chapter 1 it is said that the virtue of the operation of modelling in mathematics is that it furnishes proofs of the consistency and relative independence of mathematical theories, thus providing new knowledge. In the context of Badiou's philosophy it appears to provide evidence of the consistency of his theory – the theory of the structural dialectic – by showing how it operates within a heterogeneous field, such as a sonnet. At the same time it produces a new object of knowledge, which is the Mallarméan structural dialectic of the shipwreck. What remains to be seen, however, is how this method of modelling – at work on the local level – integrates with the method of dialectical braiding – at work at the global level – and finally what relation both methods bear to that of conditioning.

Modelling and braiding as sequencing: logics of incompletion

In Chapter 1 I claimed that the importance of modelling to Badiou is that it provides a theoretical account of the production of new knowledge as a consistent operation from one state of affairs to another state of affairs. When he employs a version of modelling within his own texts it obviously connects philosophy to diverse semantic domains and *as* it assigns different semantic values to philosophy's syntax it can cause the expansion and addition of new elements to that syntax, such as the Mallarméan motif of chance as the origin of the idea. By modelling the dialectic within the field of proletarian politics in the mid-nineteenth

century and identifying the proletariat's need to concentrate its subjective force by purging itself of revisionism Badiou extracts the concept of
destruction and then turns to Lacan to divide the Lacanian concepts of
destruction – anxiety and the superego (TS, 162). In this respect, modelling is similar to conditioning in that it produces new philosophical
concepts from an examination of heterogeneous fields. But this is
not the only effect of modelling. I said above that in his reading of
Mallarmé's sonnet Badiou attempts to add his signifiers onto a metaphorical sequence that is already constituted in the poem: he attempts to
extend and expand the work of the poem. In this manner, the philosopher mirrors the work of incompletion that I have argued is at work
in a generic truth procedure. That is, by extending the metaphorical
operations of the poem, the philosopher attempts to enlarge its boundaries and disrupt any supposed completion of the poem. Modelling a
poem thus de-totalizes it and extends it into philosophy.

But isn't this precisely what happens through conditioning? At first
sight, no: modelling is the inverse of the procedure of conditioning. In
modelling the syntax is constructed in philosophy and then tested in
diverse semantic fields such as revolutionary politics or Mallarmé's
poetry. In contrast, with conditioning it is a particular generic procedure
such as set theory that provides the syntax and philosophy provides the
semantic domain: hence 'metaontology' is a model of set theory. But
perhaps this is too puritanical an interpretation of conditioning. It is
well known that Badiou occasionally takes some liberties in his philosophical transcription of set theory and he explicitly admits this in the
notes to *Logiques des mondes*, saying 'however important the formal proof
may be, it is only here at the service of the concept'.[47] But it is not just a
matter of taking certain liberties in favour of a more comprehensible
philosophical presentation of a structure or even in favour of a different
formulation of a concept. If the task of philosophy is to construct a
space of conceptual compossibility for an entire series of generic truth
procedures, if it must circulate between a multiplicity of artistic, scientific, political and amorous conditions, it can never be perfectly faithful
to one truth procedure alone. Thus, with regard to the comparison
between modelling and conditioning, one cannot simply assert that it is
always a truth procedure alone that furnishes the syntax for the model;
sometimes it is also philosophy that provides part of the syntax, based
on its encounters with other conditions. Moreover, the most extreme
consequence of philosophy's encounter with generic truth procedures,
as I argue above, is that it can no longer draw a strict boundary between
its own practices and those of the truth procedure. If philosophy is part

theatre since the Greeks how can one securely state that it is theatre or philosophy that is the sole source of the syntax used in a procedure of modelling? What is at stake in both modelling and conditioning is the production of new knowledge through a logic of incompletion that incompletes a poem or a political movement in order to extend a sequence of thought. It is this procedure of incompletion and extension – whether it be termed modelling or conditioning – that still deserves the name of the dialectic.

What then are the consequences of this identification of Badiou's philosophical method? The first major consequence is that the sign of the lack of such method is *stasis*; that is, the stable reproduction of tried and true philosophical categories or the finishing of a dialectical sequence. Subsequently Badiou's philosophy places a Sartrean pressure upon its interlocutors: it encourages them to extend its own sequences and its logic of incompletion into other realms whether they be those of the contemporary conditions or parts of the history of philosophy. And not only does this imply the organization of reading groups, workshops, colloquiums, publications, mailing-lists, but the activation of reworked Badiousian categories in activism and art schools. In Chapter 2 I named the presence of such pressure within Badiou's philosophy *the desire for hetero-expulsion*. In the current period of Badiou's work, the period of *Being and Event*, it is not so much a question of an expulsion from philosophy into heterogeneous practices but rather a question of constructing dialectical sequences between philosophy and particular political or scientific practices. In other words, to condition philosophy is to stage enduring encounters between philosophy and certain practices – in short, as its own name dictates, philosophy needs to fall in love with the generic. It is just such an *agencement*, a linking up, an articulation of philosophy with generic truth procedures that allows a passage from philosophy through to art or politics or love. Not the least signs of the viability of such a passage are the repeated exhortations on Badiou's part to his readers to perform poetic and mathematical exercises and so to experience the peculiar consistency of an artistic or scientific practice (TS, 124, 146). This is Badiou's final twist on the Marxist doctrine of the primacy of practice.

In line with Badiou's Marxist roots our final question with regard to his method must be materialist; that is, in the end it is not the method itself which concerns us but its effects. These effects can be enumerated as follows. First, it is modelling alone that renders set-theory ontology 'concrete' by producing new knowledge of what is concrete in a particular domain. For instance, if the philosopher desires, as some commentators announce, a 'social ontology', one must start from a point of social dysfunction, such as the existence of absentee landlords and an accelerating disproportion between rising rents and stagnant or non-existent salaries. Second, modelling itself, through its procedures of assigning specific semantic values to elements of a syntax, produces consistent procedures of change; it renders change a consistent process. In doing so it increases certain people's knowledge and experience of the stakes of slow but relentless global change. Third, this knowledge is valuable since it can pass, via philosophy's encounter with generic procedures, into other practices. For instance, the philosophical reconstruction of a consistent political procedure originating in the French Revolution, once published, can help a militant in an entirely different political situation think about the stakes of their own practice. In kind, the Marxist construction of a model of political practice – though obsolete now – enabled thousands of militants to approach political history as a coherent sequence with a particular dynamic rather than as a set of isolated anarchic incidents.

In summary, the philosophical modelling of artistic, political, scientific and amorous procedures can result not only in the identification of new emergent subjects but also in their transmission as address, challenge and invention.

In the first chapter I idly entertained the possibility of placing Badiou's early literary work in relation to his philosophical oeuvre. I have had to restrict that ambition to outlining the three periods of that oeuvre. Let me finish then by merely pointing to his own literary anticipation of the predominant concerns of his philosophical work. In the prefatory remark to *Almagestes*, Badiou writes:

> This book . . . must be considered as a material introduction, an illumination of linguistic constellations and fluorescences, of baleful fascinations and influences in which we risk destroying the work, although that risk has to be run here. It is a kind of plasma, a creation of the world in which the Subject and History begin to take form . . . I can also say: the domain that I have chosen to enter by the production of a model, of a problematic object, and that I will perhaps enter upon elsewhere by means of philosophy, is that of *proliferation*, perhaps of the baroque.[48]

Badiou's mature philosophy is consecrated to the presentation of multiplicity – '*proliferation*' – and the theorization of procedures of consistent

structural change – 'creation of a world'. Through the argument I outline above it becomes clear that the production of a model is both a
presentation of a simple multiple – the two multiplicities of the syntax
and the semantic domain – and the presentation of a consistent procedure of change. To model, according to Badiou's philosophy, is thus to
think of multiplicity at the very same time as one thinks of a *sea change* in
that multiplicity.

Chapter 4

Live Badiou

Interview with Alain Badiou, Paris, December 2007

Oliver Feltham (OF): What do you mean when you describe the contemporary conjuncture by saying that it does not form a world? In the absence of a world what are the modes or principal tasks of philosophy – critique, genealogy or metaphysics? Must philosophy respond to this absence of a world by constructing its own worlds?

Alain Badiou (AB): What I mean is that the 'contemporary world' as a world formatted by the totality of capitalism does not form a world for the women and men from which it is composed. In other words, there is the abstract world of capital, but there is no world which is constituted such that all those who live within it, as fraternal inhabitants, can recognize each other. Under these conditions philosophy must say 'there is one sole world', not as a descriptive statement, but as a prescriptive statement, as what should guide the politics of emancipation today.

OF: At the very beginning of your first novel, *Trajectoire inverse: almagestes*, you speak of a model of multiplicity. One could describe the project of your philosophy as the construction of a model of multiplicity: the multiplicity of infinite worlds, and the multiplicity realized by the upsurge of a truth – the change between two worlds. Why did you turn from literature to philosophy and mathematics at the beginning of your career? Does philosophy fulfil a programme already announced in your novels?

AB: No doubt the relation between literature and philosophy is more complex. I feel philosophy to be commanded by a duty of affirmation. On the basis of the construction of a concept of truth it declares that it supports this concept, and that human animals owe it to truth to be capable of living a life worthy of its name. Literature is more buried in the immediate experience of the world, more bound to the affects and effects of infancy. It is quite clear that being known, myself, as an essentially optimist thinker, I am also quite a melancholic writer.

OF: In *The Concept of Model*, you show how the mathematical concept of model inverts the relation between what is called 'formal' and what is supposed to be 'empirical' according to Levi-Strauss' positivist epistemology. It is not formal theory that provides a model of the empirical but a particular semantic field that furnishes a model of a theory. Could one not find precisely this practice of the production of models in your reading of poetry in *Théorie du sujet*? The syntax is found in what you call the 'structural dialectic', constructed by philosophy, and that syntax consists in a series of concepts – *offsite, force, splace* – and propositions. The work of the poet then furnishes a semantic domain in which correspondences can be established between the semantic values of that domain and elements of the philosophical syntax. Subsequently one tests the model by showing how the axioms – the propositions, the concepts – hold together in their poetic model. Finally, the result of this method is not a critical reading of this or that poem, but the production of a poetic – Mallarméan – model of philosophy and thus the production of a new object of knowledge. Is the task of philosophy thus the production of new objects of knowledge? If this interpretation of your method of thinking poetry is correct, could one not understand the conditioning of philosophy in the period of *Being and Event* as an inversion of this practice? That is to say, the philosopher no longer finds her or his syntax inside philosophy but rather within a generic truth procedure: it is philosophy which produces itself as model, as a model of poetry, of politics, etc.

AB: Your idea, in any case, is ingenious. However it seems to me that the different truth procedures have different destinies with regard to this point. What you say concerning the function of the poem in *Théorie du sujet* is very striking. But can one easily extend it to the amorous procedure, for example? I think that the syntax is still, in that case, produced by philosophy, in the form of a Two which is not submitted to the classical laws of the dialectic, and whose semantic multiplicities are produced by love. Your question would have to be re-examined case by case.

OF: Given the political demands of *Le rassemblement des collectifs de sans papiers* (the coalition of the collectives of undocumented migrants), can one think, in philosophy and in politics, of a world without frontiers?

AB: There are always frontiers, but there is no necessity for these frontiers to be walls. The crucial statement – I repeat – is there is one sole world. The immanent multiplicity of this world is irreducible, but one can and must think of and practise it being a world of and for everyone.

OF: During the November 2005 events in France what disturbed the French state was what the politicians termed 'amalgams'. Several times Nicolas Sarkozy said 'let's avoid making amalgams'. These amalgams blurred the distinctions between the people who were protesting and the 'young' in general, between migrants without work permits and the sons and daughters of immigrants. On the other hand, the excluded position of undocumented migrants constitutes not so much a problem for the French state but an easy target for its repressive action – Agamben would say that bare life couples with the sovereign state. Could we not think of the initial site of a change as an incomplete multiple, or as a blurring of normally discrete categories rather than as an excluded element?

AB: Absolutely. This is what I call the potential elements of a 'grand alliance', that is to say, the disappearance, at least at a local level, of those very rigid subjective barriers upon which the State's power is based. For example, the barrier that separates young high-school or university students and the young working-class unemployed, or that which separates the ordinary workers from the 'newly arrived' prole-tariat, that is to say, workers of foreign origins. Any new political force originates in a transgression of these frontiers.

OF: In response to the reforms announced by the Minister for Educa-tion, what, in your eyes, would be a change worthy of the name in the institutions of French national education?

AB: Junior high school should be abolished: between eleven and fifteen years old all young people without exception should be integrated into productive work, with perhaps half the time spent studying, or a quarter. They will come back to full-time study once they are sixteen years old, having all acquired a tenacious 'worker' configuration. These later stud-ies will not decide their future but provide an initiation to truth pro-cedures. After which, work should be organized in such a manner that it be multi-form, that each and everyone be a 'polyvalent' worker. In actual fact, this is the communist programme. It alone has a radical sense today. Defending the 'Republican school', which is selective and elitist, has become reactionary.

OF: Is there a possible concept of ecology, and of a political ecology (rather than a political economy) in your philosophy?

AB: Let's start by stating that after 'the rights of man', the rise of 'the rights of Nature' is a contemporary form of the opium of the people. It is an only slightly camouflaged religion: the millenarian terror, concern for everything save the properly political destiny of peoples, new instruments for the control of everyday life, the obsession with hygiene, the fear of death and of catastrophes . . . It is a gigantic operation in the de-politicization of subjects. Behind it there is the idea that with strict ecological obligations one can prevent the emerging countries from competing too rapidly with the established imperial powers. The pressure exercised on China, India and Brazil has only just begun. The fact that ecology is practically consensual in our 'developed' countries is a bad sign. This is a rule: everything which is consensual is without a doubt bad for human emancipation. I am Cartesian: man is the master and possessor of nature. That has never been as true as today. The proof is that in order to save a particular species of beetle or tulip, one does not make use of nature, but of State regulations! Nature is therefore in no way a norm situated above humanity. We will inevitably make decisions according to the diversity of our interests. Ecology solely concerns me inasmuch as it can be proven that it is an intrinsic dimension of the politics of the emancipation of humanity. For the moment I do not see such proof.

OF: Where are you up to in your project of a film on Plato?

AB: In parallel with the translation of the entirety of the *Republic*, and with the monthly seminar on the contemporary force of Plato, I have begun to write the script. I will shoot, perhaps in January or February, some sketches of the very beginning with a video camera. For example, there is a scene to be shot on Rue Platon, in the 14th arrondissement; on that street there is a hostel of workers of African origins. They will hold a meeting at which one of the items on the agenda will be 'Plato'. It is this meeting that will open onto the other sequences of the film.

Notes

Chapter 1: The Althusserian years: epistemology and the production of change

1 Althusser's first four lectures can be found in the text Althusser, *Philosophie et philosophie spontanée des savants* (Paris: Editions de Maspero, 1974). The fifth lecture can be found in L. Althusser, *Écrits philosophiques et politiques, Tome II* (Paris: Stock/IMEC, 1995), 267–310. F. Regnault and M. Pecheux's text *La 'coupure épistémologique'* and E. Balibar and P. Macherey's *Expérience et Expérimentation* were promised but never saw the light of day. They can be found in draft form, as well as many notes and letters constituting the debate that took place between Althusser and his students between 1965 and 1968 on the nature of philosophy in the Althusser archives at the Abbey at Caen. For a partial reproduction of the debate see Althusser, *Écrits philosophiques et politiques, Tome II*, 313–61.

2 For the protests against the Algerian War see 'L'aveu du philosophe' on the CIEPFC website. For the ENS occupation, personal conversation with the author.

3 Badiou, *Le concept de modèle* (Paris: Maspero, 1970), 7. Re-edited with a new preface as *Le concept de modèle* (Paris: Fayard, 2007). Page numbers will be given for both editions, the number for the original edition first.

4 The English translation of this text by Zachary Luke Fraser aided by Tzuchien Tho has recently been published by Re.press Books of Melbourne: A. Badiou, *The Concept of Model*, trans. Z. L. Fraser and T. Tho (Melbourne: pre-press, 2008).

5 From 1965 to 1966 the National Centre for Pedagogical Documentation produced this series of half-hour documentaries. Badiou is clearly constrained by the format of these documentaries and he spends much of his screen time listening, smoking and briefly interrupting his illustrious elders. But in 1968 Badiou engages in an hour-long interview with Michel Serres entitled *Modèle et Structure*; Serres has just published his monumental *Le système de Leibniz et ses modèles mathématiques* and was quite well known for his work in epistemology. However, rather than simply prompting Serres with

questions as in the other interviews, Badiou presents his own arguments in tandem with Serres on the nature of scientific models and the result is a philosophical dialogue rather than an interview. The translation of the transcript of this interview, undertaken by Tzuchien Tho, is currently under consideration as part of the *Cahiers pour l'analyse* translation project under the directorship of Peter Hallward at the Centre for Modern European Philosophy at Middlesex University. Most of these interviews are available for viewing in the original at the Bibliothèque Nationale de France.

6 Badiou's only other published article of the time appears to be an extract from *Portulans*; 'L'Autorisation' in *Les temps modernes* 258, 1967, 761–89 and an essay 'Matieu' in *Derrière le miroir: 5 peintres et un sculpteur* (Paris: Maeght Editeur, 1965), 24–31.

7 L. Althusser, *Pour Marx*, re-edition of 1996 (Paris: La Découverte, 2005), 260–1. L. Althusser, *Lire le Capital*, new revised edn (Paris: Presses Universitaires de France, 1996). All subsequent references to this text will be signalled by the abbreviation LC.

8 Ibid., 176

9 See, for example, V.I. Lenin, 'Our revolution', *Lenin's Collected Works* Volume 33, 2nd English Edition (Moscow: Progress Publishers, 1965), 476–80. Also to be found on www.marxists.org. For further references see *Pour Marx*, ibid., 96 n. 15.

10 See *Pour Marx*, 209 n. 45.

11 Ibid., 198.

12 Ibid., 112, 214. RM, 457.

13 *Pour Marx*, 98.

14 See Althusser, *Philosophy of the Encounter: Later Writings, 1978–87*, trans. G. M. Goshgarian (London: Verso, 2006). In the early 1960s Althusser dismisses historical necessity but also makes a series of disparaging remarks about contingency both in its Hegelian and in its mechanist varieties – in the former, it is a purely accidental vehicle for the realization of necessity and in the latter it is a separate and unrelated or indifferent vehicle of force (*Pour Marx*, 180, 203). The dominant modality of Althusser's theory of change in this period is possibility, inasmuch as there are multiple ways in which secondary contradictions might or might not combine into a unity of rupture.

15 *Pour Marx*, 99.

16 It is indeed true that Althusser simply asserts the unity of an 'always already complex totality' without argument. See *Pour Marx*, 208.

17 Ibid., 167. Moreover, when Badiou picks up this concept of practice he claims that one can ignore the two categories of raw material and product because they are merely the limits of the process, the start point and end point as it were (RM, 454).

18 This productivist model leads Aristotle into well-documented problems concerning the definition and unity of substance due to the difficult relation

between form and matter. If he identifies substance as that which remains the same through change – the material cause – he loses unity, since only form has unity and matter consists of an infinity of accidents. If he identifies substance with the formal cause, the essence, he loses existence, since only concrete individuals exist, and they involve a problematic union of form and matter.

19 An entire tradition of process philosophy, expanded to include Bergson and Deleuze alongside Whitehead, is devoted to precisely such a model of change.

20 The argument on productivism is inspired by Tony Fry's work, specifically by his *Remakings: Ecology, Design, Philosophy* (Envirobook, 1994) and by Reiner Schurmann, *Heidegger on Being and Acting* (Indiana: Indiana University Press, 1990).

21 In his commentary on Althusser's concept of practice, Badiou focuses on transformation itself to the exclusion of the raw material and the finished product, the finite start and endpoints of change (RM, 454).

22 *Pour Marx*, 24.

23 Ibid., 25, 169. See also *Lire le Capital*, 17.

24 See Etienne Balibar, 'Le concept de coupure épistémologique de Bachelard à Althusser', *Ecrits pour Althusser* (Paris: La Découverte, 1991), 21–2. Note that against Althusser's standard classification as a 'structuralist Marxist' Balibar argues that his model of change is not structuralist inasmuch as he does not think an epistemological break as a discontinuity that separates two invariant paradigms. For Balibar this distinguishes Althusser's thought from that of both Foucault and Kuhn.

25 'The science/ideology opposition is developed as a process' (RM, 450).

26 Badiou remains indebted in this period to this classic conception of science as a form of automaton, a discourse without a soul. However he does note that another conception is possible, specifically in the shape of Michel Serres' argument that mathematics, in the early twentieth century, engaged in its own epistemological investigation of its practice. See '(Re)commencement', 453 n. 21, which refers to M. Serres, 'La Querelle des anciens et modernes en mathématiques', *Critique*, no. 198, Nov. 1963.

27 See note 1. See Althusser, *Écrits philosophiques et politiques, Tome II*, 360–1.

28 J. A. Miller, 'La suture: éléments de la logique du signifiant', reprinted in Miller, *Un début dans la vie* (Paris: Le cabinet des lettres, 2002). See the English translation by Jacqueline Rose, 'Suture: Elements for a Logic of the Signifier' in *Screen* 18, Winter 1978 which is somewhat badly reproduced within the online journal *The Symptom* at lacan.com. Badiou's article forms part of a translation programme for much of the *Cahiers pour l'Analyse* material under Peter Hallward's direction at the Centre for Modern European Philosophy at Middlesex University.

29 G. Frege, *The Foundations of Arithmetic*, 2nd revised edn, trans. J. L. Austin

(Northwestern University Press, 1980). Note that Bertrand Russell sent an objection to Frege's definition of number in a letter that obliged Frege, on the point of publication, to entirely rework his logical foundation of arithmetic. We will revisit this point in Chapter 3 with reference to the definition of sets. The letter – one of the briefest and most explosive texts in the history of philosophy – and Frege's response is to be found in J. van Heijenoort (ed.), *From Frege to Gödel: A Source Book in Mathematical Logic, 1879–1931* (Harvard: Harvard University Press, 2002).

30 Frege, *The Foundations of Arithmetic*, §68.

31 Ibid.

32 For a clear exegesis of Frege's argument, see Claude Imbert's introduction to her translation of the text; G. Frege, *Les fondements de l'arithmétique* (Paris: Seuil, 1969), 11–104. See also Badiou's concise exegesis in Chapter 2 of his *Le nombre et les nombres* (Paris: Seuil, 1990) translated by Robin Mackay as *Number and Numbers* (London: Polity, 2008).

33 Frege, *Foundations*, §79.

34 J. A. Miller, 'La suture', 100.

35 Miller claims that in Frege's argument the only possible support for the non-existence of non-self-identical objects is Leibniz's principle of identity as cited by Frege in the lead-up to his definition of number: 'those things are identical which can be substituted for each other without loss of truth' (Frege, §65). However, in order to function as a premise, this principle must be transformed into quite a different proposition: 'there is truth, therefore all objects are self-identical'. Miller does identify Frege's primary commitment to the existence of truth but he does not acknowledge this implicit transformation of the principle of identity.

36 Ibid, 107.

37 Ibid., 96–7.

38 See Badiou, 'The Cultural Revolution: The Last Revolution?', trans. B. Bosteels in *Positions East Asia Culture Critique: Special Issue Alain Badiou and Cultural Revolution*, Vol. 13, No. 3, Winter 2005, 481–514.

39 *Le nombre et les nombres*, 42.

40 For Badiou's reference to Bachelard's position on scientific instrumentality as materialized theory as a premise of his own investigations see *Le concept de modèle*, 53–4. See Bachelard, *Le nouvel esprit scientifique* (Paris: Presses Universitaires de France, 1934), 14.

41 See also *Pour Marx*, 40, 239.

42 See BE, 486, note to page 60.

43 See MM, 151 n. 3 on sense as an operator of dissimulation.

44 Earlier in this article, during his exegesis of Gödel's undecidable propositions with regard to their non-placement in the third mechanism of derivation, Badiou states in apparent reference to Miller 'one cannot argue that tearing apart (*déchirure*) or compulsive iteration are the inevitable price of closure'. However, this remark can also be quite easily read as furnishing the

elements for a critique of Derrida's use of Gödel's undecidability theorems. See 'Marque et manqué', 153.

45 See M. Blanchot, *The Space of Literature* (Lincoln: University of Nebraska Press, 1982).

46 *Le concept de modèle* (2007), 34–6.

47 *Pour Marx*, 239.

48 See Balibar, 'Le concept de coupure épistémologique de Bachelard à Althusser', 19.

49 See Badiou, *Logiques des mondes* (Paris: Seuil, 2006), 561–2 on Badiou's relation to Kant.

50 Badiou, 'Qu'est-ce que Louis Althusser entend par « philosophie »?' in S. Lazarus (ed.), *Politique et philosophie dans l'oeuvre de Louis Althusser* (Paris: Presses Universitaires de France, 1992), 32.

51 One wonders why those who compose such laments do not simply turn to Niklas Luhmann's social systems theory which does provide a 'relational' social ontology.

52 This conception seems to be closer to Bachelard's concept of an epistemological break than Althusser's since for Bachelard a break is less an epoch-defining macro-event that can be dated but rather a process that occurs within every scientific laboratory and text in the continual construction of scientific knowledge See *Le nouvel esprit scientifique*, 179 on the perpetual revision of error.

53 In this text Badiou presents a far more intricate picture of the relation between mathematics and philosophy, than that found in his later doctrine of conditions. This is no surprise given his material: the development of mathematical logic in the early twentieth century in which certain authors – Frege, Gödel, Russell, Carnap, Quine – figure as both philosophers and logicians if not mathematicians.

54 For instance, Badiou refers to Quine's work on constructing a logic of stratification which would reduce the multiple strata of logic by indexing them onto one strata. In Badiou's eyes the multiplicity of strata are irreducible and so such attempts are doomed to failure. See 'Marque et Manque', 161 n. 16.

55 The continuum hypothesis, originally advanced by Cantor, posits that the cardinality of the powerset of the first infinite set, the aleph, is that of the successor to the aleph. See *Being and Event*, 504.

56 In the psychoanalytic framework within which Lacan developed this gnomic aphorism, the real is conceived as an obstacle that causes symbolic protocols of behaviour or language to differentiate and multiply, whereas reality is whatever allows an unconscious protocol to operate without obstruction. The real is thus a direct development of Freud's definition of the reality principle as an extension of the pleasure principle. See J. Lacan, *Seminar 11: The Four Fundamental Concepts of Psychoanalysis*, trans. A. Sheridan (London: Penguin, 1994), 167.

57 Badiou devotes an entire development on the organs of a body of change to the exegesis of Galois' remark in *Logiques des mondes*, 493–7.

58 As the source of the term *refonte* Badiou refers to François Regnault's lecture (in Althusser's aforementioned course) on the notion of epistemological break. See 'Subversion Infinitésimale', 120 n. 1.

59 Badiou in a recent interview dismisses the seriousness of this judgement by claiming that not only was this kind of diagnosis widespread at the time – the accusation of 'theoreticism' was bandied about – but that given the political context he was entirely in agreement with it and actually formed part of the editorial collective that wrote the 'warning'. The editorial collective softens its line somewhat by allowing that certain conjunctures require purely philosophical work, citing Lenin's critique of empiricism. See the interview 'The Concept of Model 40 years Later', in Badiou, *The Concept of Model*, 79–104.

Chapter 2: Maoism and the dialectic

1 *Théorie de la contradiction* (Paris: Maspero, 1975), 2.

2 The corpus for a full study of this period of Badiou's work consists of the following texts: *Contribution au problème de la construction d'un parti marxiste-léniniste de type nouveau*, in collaboration with the Parti socialiste unifié (Paris: Maspero, 1970); *Théorie de la contradiction* (Paris: Maspero, 1975); *De l'idéologie*, in collaboration with F. Balmès (Paris: Maspero, 1976); 'Le Mouvement ouvrier révolutionnaire contre le syndicalisme', published by the Groupe pour la fondation de l'Union des communistes de France Marxistes Léninistes Maoïstes (Marseilles: Editions Potemkine, 1976); *Le Noyau rationnel de la dialectique hégélienne*, commentary on a text by Zhang Shiying in collaboration with L. Mossot and J. Bellassen (Paris: Maspero, 1977); 'Le Flux et le parti (dans les marges de *L'Anti-Oedipe*)' in A. Badiou and S. Lazarus (eds), *La Situation actuelle sur le front de la philosophie*, Cahiers Yenan no. 4 (Paris: Maspero, 1977); *L'Écharpe rouge. Romanopéra*. (Paris: Maspero, 1979); 'Jean Paul Sartre' (Paris: Potemkine, 1980); *Théorie du sujet*. (Paris: Seuil, 1982).

3 Bruno Bosteels is currently undertaking the translation of *Théorie du sujet* for Continuum Books. See also his excellent study of Badiou's Maoism and post-Maoism 'Post-Maoism: Badiou and Politics' in the indispensable *Special Issue on Alain Badiou and the Cultural Revolution of Positions* (see Chapter 1, n. 39) which includes a full bibliography of the Groupe pour la fondation de l'Union des communistes de France Marxistes Léninistes Maoïstes (UCFML, the political group Badiou belonged to in this period). See also B. Bosteels, 'Alain Badiou's Theory of the Subject Part I: The Recommencement of Dialectical Materialism?' in *Pli*, Vol. 12 (2001), 200–29, and 'Alain Badiou's Theory of the Subject: The Recommencement of Dialectical Materialism? (Part II)' in *Pli*, Vol. 13 (2002), 173–208. Alberto Toscano also writes on

this period of Badiou's work though his real centre of interest is what he terms the 'transitional period' between 1982 and 1988, the period of *Peut-on penser la politique?* (1985). See A. Toscano, 'Communism as Separation' in P. Hallward (ed.), *Think Again: Alain Badiou and the Future of Philosophy* (London: Continuum, 2004), 138–49, and Alberto Toscano, 'Marxism Expatriated: Alain Badiou's Turn' in Jacques Bidet and Stathis Kouvelakis (eds) *Critical Companion to Contemporary Marxism* (Leiden: E. J. Brill, 2007), 529–48. See also Sophie Gosselin's article on *Théorie du sujet* 'La Parole Manifeste' in B. Besana and O. Feltham (eds), *Écrits autour de la pensée d'Alain Badiou* (Paris: Harmattan, 2007), 171–85. See Jason Barker, *An Introduction to Alain Badiou* (London: Pluto Press, 2002).

4 G. W. F. Hegel, *The Science of Logic*, trans. A. V. Miller (New York: Humanity Books, 1969), 825.

5 The passage from *Théorie de la contradiction* containing this commentary is translated by A. Toscano in the *Special Issue* of *Positions* mentioned in note 3, 669–77.

6 See T. Tho and Z. L. Fraser's interview with Badiou included in *The Concept of Model*, ibid.

7 From the point of view of Badiou's later set-theory ontology, he illegitimately conflates belonging – the question of unity – with ordering here.

8 One of the foci of Bruno Besana's comparative work between Deleuze and Badiou is precisely the vexed question of the 'genesis' of situations. See his 'L'être de l'événement' in *Écrits autour de la pensée d'Alain Badiou*, 125–30. This is also one of Felix Ensslin's concerns.

9 J. Lacan, *Seminar 11: The Four Fundamental Concepts of Psychoanalysis*, 6.

10 Ibid., 29. Lacan refers to Miller's question at the beginning of the 29 January 1964 session. The questions and answers from the 22 January 1964 session are missing.

11 Hegel, *The Science of Logic*, 521–3.

12 11 July 2007.

13 Cameron Tonkinwise of Parsons New School of Design argues that in order to build sustainable energy systems old energy infrastructures must be destroyed: infrastructures that literally lock us in concrete into unsustainable futures. See C. Tonkinwise, 'Is Design Finished? Dematerialisation and Changing Things', *Design Philosophy Papers*, Vol. 3 (2004), 1–16.

14 Jacques Lacan, *Seminar I: Freud's Papers on Technique*, trans. John Forrester (Cambridge: Cambridge University Press, 1988), 199.

15 On the identification of a generic truth procedure in indigenous Australian politics, see my article 'Singularity happening in politics: the Aboriginal Tent Embassy, Canberra 1972', *Communication and Cognition*, Vol. 37 No. 1, 2004, 225–45.

16 One could object that this is also what he does later on in having recourse to set theory and the generic set – yes, already in *Théorie du sujet*! – but

precisely the drama of set theory is that it allows Badiou to think structural heterogeneity *without exiting from the quantitative order.*

17 Thus when Bruno Bosteels sets out to critique miraculous and absolutist interpretations of Badiou's philosophy he is in fact critiquing their exclusive focus on a tendency that is internal to Badiou's own philosophy; a tendency I call the 'eagle'. Any thorough interpretation of Badiou must recognize the other tendencies in his thinking of change. See Bosteels, 'Post-Maoism: Badiou and Politics', 581.

18 J. Lacan, Seminar XXIII: R.S.I, *Ornicar?* No. 3.

19 Ex-sistence is one of Lacan's neologisms, often used to designate the impact of the real as vanished cause; that is, the position and agency of something – such as the *objet petit a*, the object cause of desire – which is absent from the symbolic order and yet has effects upon that order.

20 In J. Lacan, *Écrits*, trans. B. Fink (New York: W. W. Norton, 2007), 161–75.

21 The key text that begins to draw philosophical conclusions from this position on immigrant workers is *Peut-on penser la politique?* in which Badiou dates his work with the *sans-papiers* as beginning in 1972, p. 74. For documents concerning this work see Alain Badiou, *Political Writings*, ed. and trans. N. Power and A. Toscano (New York: Columbia University Press, *forthcoming* 2009).

22 This entire argument is developed in a paper 'The Pleasures of Incompletion: France and her Ex-colonies' given at the Politics and Culture Research Seminar, New York University in France, January 2007.

23 How many generations must pass before one is no longer an immigrant in the eyes of the French state?

24 A retired worker of Algerian origins, 71 years old, cited in Eric Marlière, 'Les habitants des quartiers: adversaires ou solidaires des émeutiers' in En L. Mucchieli and V. Le Gaziou (eds), *Quand les banlieues brûlent: retour sur les émeutes de novembre 2005* (Paris: le Découverte, 2006), 76.

25 I owe my interest in this question to Alberto Toscano's excellent investigation of the question of reactive subjects in Badiou's work in the context of the theorization of the ideology of Al Qaeda and the inadequacy of the concept of 'islamofascism' or 'islamic fundamentalism' to explain the phenomenon. See A. Toscano, 'The Bourgeois and the Islamist, or, The Other Subjects of Politics' in P. Ashton, A. J. Bartlett and J. Clemens (eds), *The Praxis of Alain Badiou* (Melbourne: Re.press, 2006), 339–66.

26 N. Sarkozy; 'La France ne peut pas accueillir toute la misère du monde. Nous avons le droit de choisir qui est le bienvenu' (France cannot accommodate all the misery of the world. We have the right to choose who is welcome), televised debate with Segolène Royal, 2 May 2007, TF1.

Chapter 3: Set-theory ontology and the modelling of change

1 *Peut-on penser la politique* (Paris: Seuil, 1985) is a text that originated in papers Badiou gave at two conferences on philosophy and politics organized by Jean-Luc Nancy and Philippe Lacoue-Labarthe, which were published – without including Badiou's texts – as *Rejouer le politique* (Paris: Galilée, 1981) et *Le retrait du politique* (Paris: Galilée, 1983). An exclusive selection of Nancy and Lacoue-Labarthe's contributions to these collections was translated in S. Sparks (ed.), *Retreating the political* (London: Routledge, 1997). Badiou's text is currently being translated by Bruno Bosteels: A. Badiou, *Can Politics Be Thought?* followed by *Of An Obscure Disaster: The End of the Truth of State* (Durham: Duke University Press, *forthcoming*).

2 Daniel Bensaid, 'Alain Badiou and the Miracle of the Event', in P. Hallward (ed.), *Think Again: Alain Badiou and the Future of Philosophy*, 104.

3 This is an expansion of the *De l'idéologie* position that states that it is only during a political conflict that ideology divides and presents its multiplicity (DI, 37).

4 J-L. Nancy, *La communauté désoeuvrée* (Paris: C. Bourgois, 1986), Philippe Lacoue-Labarthe, *La fiction du politique* (Paris: C. Bourgois, 1988).

5 G. W. Leibniz, 'Letter to Arnauld April 30 1687', *Philosophical Writings*, trans. J. M. Morris, (London: Dent & Sons, 1934), 72.

6 Heidegger, *Being and Time*, Trans. Macquarrie & Robinson (Oxford: Blackwell, 1962), 26. In a later essay, 'The Question of Being Today' (in *Court traité d'ontologie transitoire*), Badiou reveals one of his chief references in Heidegger's work to be 'Sketches for a History of Being as Metaphysics' and cites it in support of his recasting of the Heideggerean problematic. See M. Heidegger, *The End of Philosophy*, trans. J. Stambaugh (Chicago: University of Chicago Press, 2003), 55–74.

7 Ray Brassier is quite correct to remark that it is not clear on what basis Badiou derives his Lacanian thesis 'there is Oneness', and so, despite its appearance in a philosophical prolegomena to the identification of mathematics with set theory, its only basis can be set theory itself and its manipulation of unified sets in the form of variables. See R. Brassier, 'Presentation as anti-phenomenon in Alain Badiou's *Being and Event*', *Continental Philosophy Review* 39 (2006), 59–77.

8 See Anindya Bhattacharya's development of a 'work-around' for Badiou's problem with the Axiom of Foundation and his doctrine of neutral, natural and historical situations (as yet unpublished). See Beau Madison Mount's work on the constructible universe in set theory in 'The Cantorian Revolution: Alain Badiou and the Philosophy of Set Theory', *Polygraph* 17, 2005, 41–91. See Zachary Luke Fraser's 'The Law of the Subject: Alain Badiou, Luitsen Brouwer and the Kripkean Analyses of Forcing and the Heyting Calculus', in P. Ashton, A. J. Bartlett, and J. Clemens (eds), *The Praxis of Alain Badiou*, 23–70.

9 A. Badiou, *Le concept de modèle* (2007), 34–6.

10 Donald Davidson, *Essays on Actions and Events* (Oxford: Clarendon Press, 1980).

11 See Eduardo Acotto's 'L'ontologie du monde perdu' for a bracing critique of Badiou's ontology in the name of analytic metaphysics in *Écrits autour de la pensée d'Alain Badiou*, 83–100.

12 If it were possible to construct a genealogy within Badiou's oeuvre for this concept of an ineluctable ground for the existence of a political state or mechanism of re-grouping, one would refer back to Althusser's conception of irreducibility of the science–ideology relationship.

13 Badiou, 'Raisonnement hautement spéculatif sur le concept de démocratie', *Abrégé de métapolitique* (Paris: Seuil, 1998), 91. My translation.

14 Ibid., 91.

15 There is a well-known problem with the distinction between natural and historical multiples in Badiou's metaontology. On the one hand, the ordinal sets are said to write the being of natural situations. On the other hand, the axiom of foundation specifies that every set contains an evental-site, an element whose intersection with the initial set is void; thus all sets write the being of historical situations. Badiou gets around this difficulty with an awkward use of Heidegger's ontological difference: in the situation of ontology, all sets are founded by the void-set; in ontic or non-ontological situations, certain situations are historical if they are founded by non-void singular multiples. Note that Anindya Bhattacharya, as noted above, has developed a work around for this difficulty.

16 F. Nietzsche, *Genealogy of Morals*, II, 12, trans. W. Kaufman and R. J. Hollingdale (Vintage Books, 1989).

17 Strictly speaking this would be a Megaric deviation of the Aristotelian conception of production according to which potentiality only exists in the moment of being actualized. See Aristotle's refutation of the Megarians in *Metaphysics* IX, 3.

18 See R. Brassier, 'Nihil Unbound: Remarks on Subtractive Ontology and Thinking Capitalism', in *Think Again*, ibid., 50–8.

19 See J. Lacan, *Seminar 11: The Four Fundamental Concepts of Psychoanalysis*, trans. A. Sheridan (London: Penguin, 1979), 52–63.

20 See B. Formis, 'Event and Ready-made: Delayed Sabotage', *Communication and Cognition: Miracles do Happen: Essays on Alain Badiou*, Vol. 37 No. 1, 2004, 247–61.

21 Virgil, *The Aeneid*, trans. R. Fagles (New York: Viking Books, 2006), 62–4. Bk I, l.550–96 (456–93).

22 See Bruno Besana, 'L'événement de l'être' in *Écrits autour de la pensée d'Alain Badiou*, 125–130.

23 Badiou, *Logiques des mondes*, 381.

24 Peter Hallward makes a connection between the generic multiple and a form of sovereignty in the title of an early article on Badiou: 'Generic

Sovereignty: The Philosophy of Alain Badiou', *Angelaki* 3 (3), 1998, 87–110. See Badiou on the problem of decisionism in the interview at the back of A. Badiou, *Infinite Thought*, ed. and trans. J. Clemens and O. Feltham (London: Continuum, 2003), 172–3.

25 *Logiques des mondes*, 381. These difficulties, implicitly acknowledged in *Being and Event*, concern the Axiom of Foundation and the consequent belonging of a type of eventual-site – the void-set – to every situation which undoes Badiou's regionalization of being (see n. 15). See *Being and Event*, 188–9.

26 L. Althusser, *Pour Marx*, 110.

27 Further examination of this point would require an analysis of the theory of points in *Logiques des mondes*. The question is whether or not it constitutes, in Badiou's own terms, a 'coup de droit', a objectivizing correction of what he now diagnoses as an excessive emphasis on the subjective side of generic truth procedures in *Being and Event*. See Badiou's intervention on 24 November 2006 during the *Autour de Logiques des mondes* conference on the ENS *Diffusion des savoirs* site.

28 This is Barbara Formis' argument; she develops it in the article cited in note 17 and in far greater detail but with a different conceptual framework in her PhD, 'Esthétique des gestes ordinaires dans l'art contemporain', supervisor Prof. Anne Moeglin-Decroix, Department of Philosophy, Sorbonne University Paris I, December 2007, unpublished.

29 A. Badiou, *Ethics*, trans. P. Hallward (London: Verso, 2001), 73.

30 Ibid., 86.

31 Ibid., 85.

32 See §678 in F. Nietzsche, *The Will to Power*, trans. W. Kaufmann and R. J. Hollingdale (New York: Vintage Books, 1968), 359.

33 Badiou, *Ethics*, 46.

34 For his critique of Deleuze's ontology see Badiou's *Deleuze: The Clamor of Being*, trans. L. Burchill (Minneapolis: University of Minnesota Press, 1999).

35 Carlos Frade organized the October 2007 colloquium 'Badiou's Europe vs Nietzsche's Europe: Emancipatory Politics and Great Politics' at the Institute for Social, Cultural and Policy Research at the University of Salford, Manchester.

36 See Badiou's critique of Nietzsche's archi-political stance in 'Casser en deux l'histoire du monde', *Le Perroquet* No. 37 Décembre 1992, 5–25. Much of this text has been translated by Alberto Toscano under the title 'Who is Nietzsche?' in *Pli* 11, 2001, 1–11.

37 See P. Osborne, 'Badiou's Neo-classicism', *Radical Philosophy* 142, March/April 2007, 19–29. S. Žižek, 'The Politics of Truth, or, Alain Badiou as a Reader of St Paul' in *The Ticklish Subject* (London: Verso, 1999), 127–70. Žižek's position on Badiou has been modified and nuanced in subsequent texts.

38 A. Badiou, 'Saisissement, Desaisie, Fidelité' [Capture, Abandon, Fidelity], *Les Temps Modernes: Temoins de Sartre Vol. 1*, Oct.–Dec. 1990, Nos. 531–3, 14.

39 I examine the consequences of drawing such conclusions in 'An Explosive Genealogy: Theatre, Philosophy and the Art of Presentation' in *The Praxis of Alain Badiou*, 247–64.

40 For this accusation see P. Osborne, 'Badiou's Neo-classicism', 22.

41 A. Badiou, *Infinite Thought*, 178.

42 See A. Badiou, 'One, Multiple, Multiplicities' in R. Brassier and A. Toscano (eds), *Theoretical Writings* (London: Continuum, 2004), 78.

43 *Infinite Thought*, 171.

44 This is an argument made by Quentin Meillassoux in his excellent article 'Nouveauté et événement' in C. Ramond (ed.) *Alain Badiou: penser le multiple* (Paris: Harmattan, 2002), 39–64.

45 It is not Badiou but Georges Canguilhem who originally states 'philosophy does not produce truths' in his interview with Badiou in 1965. This statement occasioned no little discussion in the roundtable between Raymond Aron, Alain Badiou, Georges Canguilhem, Michel Foucault, Jean Hyppolite and Paul Ricoeur which concluded the series of interviews.

46 For one of the most rigorous formulations of the stakes of philosophical reading of literature see both Derrida's critique of Lacan's reading of Poe in 'Le Facteur de la vérité' in J. Derrida, *The Postcard* (Chicago: University of Chicago Press, 1987) 413–96 and Derrida's own reading of Mallarmé in 'The Double Session', Dissemination, trans. B. Johnson (Chicago: University of Chicago Press, 1981), 172–286.

47 In this passage Badiou is referring to mathematically based critiques of his formulation of the postulate of materialism, an essential element in his anchoring of the logics of worlds to the set theory ontology of those worlds. See *Logiques des mondes*, 559.

48 A. Badiou, *Trajectoire inverse: Almagestes* (Paris: Seuil, 1964), 9.

Bibliography

Selected works by Alain Badiou

These are arranged in chronological order, grouped according to the periods of Badiou's work treated in each of the three chapters. English translations of texts are noted after each entry if applicable. For a complete bibliography readers are asked to refer to either P. Hallward's bibliography in *Think Again: Alain Badiou and the Future of Philosophy*, 259–66; or Paul Ashton, A. J. Bartlett and J. Clemens' bibliography in *The Praxis of Alain Badiou*, 393–409, especially for a full list of Badiou's articles in the later period.

Period of Chapter 1

Almagestes: Trajectoire Inverse, novel (Paris: Seuil, 1964).
Portulans: Trajectoire Inverse, novel (Paris: Seuil, 1967).
'Matieu' in *Derrière le miroir: 5 peintres et un sculpteur* (Paris: Maeght Editeur, 1965), 24–31.
'L'autonomie du processus historique', *Cahiers Marxistes-Léninistes*, Paris: École Normale Supérieure, Nos. 12–13, juillet–octobre 1966, 77–89.
'Le (Re)commencement de la dialectique matérialiste', *Critique*, Tome XXIII, No. 240, Mai 1967, 438–67.
'L'Autorisation', *Les temps modernes*, No. 258, 1967, 761–89.
'La subversion infinitésimale', *Cahiers pour l'analyse*, No. 9, Juin (Paris: le Graphe, 1968), 118–37.
'Marque et Manque', *Cahiers pour l'analyse*, No. 10, Jan (Paris: le Graphe, 1969), 150–73.
Le concept de modèle (Paris: Maspero, 1970); re-edited with a new preface as *Le concept de modèle* (Paris: Fayard, 2007); *The Concept of Model*, trans. Z. L. Fraser and T. Tho (Melbourne: Re.press, forthcoming 2008).

Period of Chapter 2

Contribution au problème de la construction d'un parti marxiste-léniniste de type nouveau, in collaboration with the Parti socialiste unifié (Paris: Maspero, 1970).

Théorie de la contradiction (Paris: Maspero, 1975).

De l'idéologie, in collaboration with F. Balmès (Paris: Maspero, 1976).

'Le Mouvement ouvrier révolutionnaire contre le syndicalisme', published by the Groupe pour la fondation de l'Union des communistes de France Marxistes Léninistes Maoïstes (Marseilles: Editions Potemkine, 1976).

Le Noyau rationnel de la dialectique hégélienne, commentary on a text by Zhang Shiying in collaboration with L. Mossot and J. Bellassen (Paris: Maspero, 1977).

'Le Flux et le parti (dans les marges de *L'Anti–Oedipe*)' in A. Badiou and S. Lazarus (eds), *La Situation actuelle sur le front de la philosophie*, Cahiers Yenan No. 4 (Paris: Maspero, 1977); 'The Flux and the Party: in the Margins of Anti–Oedipus', trans. L. Balladur and S. Krysl, *Polygraph* Nos. 15–16, 2004, 75–92.

La 'Contestation' dans le P.C.F. (Marseilles: Potemkine, 1978).

L'Écharpe rouge. Romanopéra, novel/libretto (Paris: Maspero, 1979).

Jean-Paul Sartre (Paris: Potemkine, 1980). Reprinted in Petit Panthéon Portatif (Paris: La Fabrique, 2008).

Théorie du sujet (Paris: Seuil, 1982); *Theory of the subject*, trans. B. Bosteels (London: Continuum, forthcoming).

Period of Chapter 3

Peut–on penser la politique? (Paris: Seuil, 1985); *Can Politics be Thought?* followed by *Of an Obscure Disaster: The End of the Truth of the State*, trans. B. Bosteels (Durham: Duke University Press, forthcoming).

L'être et l'événement (Paris: Seuil, 1988); *Being and Event*, trans. O. Feltham (London: Continuum, 2006).

Manifeste pour la philosophie (Paris: Seuil, 1989); *Manifesto for Philosophy*, trans. N. Madarasz (Albany: SUNY Press, 1999).

Le nombre et les nombres (Paris: Seuil, 1990); *Number and Numbers*, trans. R. Mackay (London: Polity, forthcoming 2008).

Rhapsodie pour le théâtre (Paris: Le Spectateur français, 1990).

'Saisissement, Desaisie, Fidelité', *Les Temps Modernes: Temoins de Sartre Vol. 1*, Nos. 531–3, Oct.–Dec. 1990, 14–22.

D'un désastre obscur: sur le fin de la vérité de l'état (Paris: Éditions de l'aube, 1991); *Of an Obscure Disaster: The End of the Truth of the State* in *Can Politics be Thought?*, trans. B. Bosteels (Durham: Duke University Press, forthcoming).

'Qu'est–ce que Louis Althusser entend par "philosophie?" ' in S. Lazarus (ed.), *Politique et philosophie dans l'oeuvre de Louis Althusser* (Paris: Presses Universitaires de France, 1992), 29–45. Reprinted in Petit Panthéon Portatif (Paris: La Fabrique, 2008).

'Casser en deux l'histoire du monde', *Le Perroquet*, No. 37, Décembre 1992, 5–25.

Conditions (Paris: Seuil, 1992); selections have been translated in *Theoretical Writings* and *Infinite Thought*.

L'éthique: essai sur le conscience du mal (Paris: Hatier, 1993); *Ethics: an Essay on the understanding of Evil*, trans. P. Hallward (London: Verso, 2001).

'Silence, Solipsisme, Sanctité: l'antiphilosophie de Wittgenstein', *BARCA! Poésie, Politique, Psychanalyse*, No. 3., 1994, 13–54.

Ahmed le subtil, play (Arles: Actes Sud, 1994).

Ahmed se fâche followed by *Ahmed philosophe*, plays (Arles: Actes Sud, 1995).

Citrouilles, play (Arles: Actes Sud, 1995).

Beckett: l'incrévable désir (Paris: Hachette, 1995); *On Beckett*, trans. N. Power, A. Toscano with B. Bosteels (London: Clinamen Press, 2003).

Gilles Deleuze: la clameur de l'être (Paris: Hachette, 1997); *Deleuze: the Clamor of Being*, trans. L. Burchill (Minneapolis: University of Minnesota Press, 2000).

Saint Paul: la fondation de l'universalisme (Paris: Presses Universitaires de France, 1997); *Saint Paul: The Foundation of Universalism*, trans. R. Brassier (Stanford: Stanford University Press, 2003).

Calme bloc ici-bas, novel (Paris: P.O.L., 1997).

Court traité d'ontologie transitoire (Paris: Seuil, 1998); *Briefings on Existence: a Short Treatise on Transitory Ontology*, trans. N. Madarasz (Albany: State University of New York Press, 2006).

Abrégé de Metapolitique (Paris: Seuil, 1998); *Metapolitics*, trans. J. Barker (London: Verso, 2004).

Petit manuel de l'inesthétique (Paris: Seuil, 1998); *Handbook of Inaesthetics*, trans. A. Toscano (Stanford: Stanford University Press, 2003).

Circonstances 1: Kosovo, 11 septembre, Chirac/Le Pen (Paris: Léo Scheer, 2003); in *Polemics*, ed. and trans. S. Corcoran (London: Verso, 2006).

Infinite Thought: truth and the return to philosophy, ed. and trans. J. Clemens and O. Feltham (London: Continuum, 2003).

Antiphilosophie de Wittgenstein (Paris: Nous, 2004).

Theoretical Writings, ed. and trans. R. Brassier and A. Toscano (London: Continuum, 2004).

Le siècle (Paris: Seuil, 2004); *The Century*, trans. A. Toscano (London: Polity, 2007).

Circonstances 2: Iraq, foulard, Allemagne/France (Paris: Léo Scheer, 2004); in *Polemics*, ed. and trans. S. Corcoran (London: Verso, 2006).

Circonstances 3: portées du mot 'juif' (Paris: Léo Scheer, 2005); in *Polemics*, ed. and trans. S. Corcoran (London: Verso, 2006).

'The Cultural Revolution: The Last Revolution?', trans. B. Bosteels in *Positions East Asia Culture Critique: Special Issue Alain Badiou and Cultural Revolution*, Vol. 13, No. 3, Winter 2005.

Logiques des mondes (Paris: Seuil, 2006); *Logics of Worlds*, trans. A. Toscano (London: Continuum, forthcoming).

Circonstances 4: de quoi Sarkozy est–il le nom? (Paris: Nouvelles Éditions Lignes, 2007). *Petit Panthéon Portatif* (Paris: La Fabrique, 2008).

Political Writings, ed. and trans. N. Power and A. Toscano (New York: Columbia University Press, forthcoming 2009).

Introductions, monographs and collections of essays on Badiou

Barker, J., *An Introduction to Alain Badiou* (London: Pluto Press, 2002).

Besana, B. and Feltham, O. (eds), *Écrits autour de la pensée d'Alain Badiou* (Paris: Harmattan, 2007). Calcagno, A. *Badiou and Derrida* (London: Continuum, 2007).

Hallward, P., *Badiou: Subject to Truth* (Minneapolis: University of Minnesota Press, 2003).

Hallward, P. (ed.), *Think Again: Alain Badiou and the Future of Philosophy* (London: Continuum, 2004). Hewlett, M. Badiou Balibar, Ranciere (London: Continuum, 2007).

Ramond, C. (ed.), *Alain Badiou: penser le multiple* (Paris: Harmattan, 2002).

Riera, G., *Alain Badiou: Philosophy and its Conditions* (Albany: SUNY Press, 2005).

Tarby, F., *Philosophie d'Alain Badiou* (Paris: Harmattan, 2005).

Journal issues on Badiou

Ashton, P., Bartlett, A. J. and Clemens, J. (eds), *The Praxis of Alain Badiou* (Melbourne: Re.press, 2006), reprint of *The Praxis of Alain Badiou* double issue of *Cosmos and History: The Journal of Natural and Social Philosophy*, Vol. 2, Nos 1 and 2, 2006. Available online.

Barlow, T. (ed.), *Positions East Asia Culture Critique: Special Issue Alain Badiou and Cultural Revolution*, Vol. 13, No. 3, Winter 2005. Beaulieu, A. and Calcagno, A. (eds), *Symposium: Special Issue Alain Badiou, Being, Events and Philosophy*.

Hoens, D. (ed.), *The True is Always New: Essays on Alain Badiou*, special issue of *Communication and Cognition*, Vol. 37, Nos. 1/2, 2003.

Hoens, D. (ed.), *Miracles do Happen: Essays on Alain Badiou*, special issue of *Communication and Cognition*, Vol. 37, Nos. 3/4, 2004.

Wilkens, M. (ed.), *The Philosophy of Alain Badiou*, special issue of *Polygraph*, 17, 2005.

Cahiers du Collège International de Philosophie No. 8., 1989.

Also look for single essays either by Badiou or on Badiou in the following journals: *Angelaki, Collapse, Cosmos and History, Lacanian Ink, La Distance Politique, Multitudes, Paragraph, Pli, Radical Philosophy, Rue Descartes, S, Les Temps Modernes, Theory and Event.*

Secondary material

Althusser, L., *Pour Marx*, re-edition of 1996 (Paris: La Découverte, 2005).

——— *Lire le Capital*, new rev. edn (Paris: Presses Universitaires de France, 1996).
——— *Philosophie et philosophie spontanée des savants* (Paris: Editions de Maspero, 1974).
——— *Philosophy of the Encounter: Later Writings, 1978–87*, trans. G.M. Goshgarian (London: Verso, 2006).
——— *Écrits philosophiques et politiques, Tome II* (Paris: Stock/IMEC, 1995).
Bachelard, G., *Le nouvel esprit scientifique* (Paris: Presses Universitaires de France, 1934).
——— *La formation de l'esprit scientifique* (Paris: Vrin, 1938).
——— *L'activité rationaliste de la physique contemporaine* (Paris: Presses Universitaires de France, 1951).
Balibar, E., *Écrits pour Althusser* (Paris: La Découverte, 1991).
Bosteels, B., 'Alain Badiou's Theory of the Subject Part I: The Recommencement of Dialectical Materialism?', *Pli*, Vol. 12, 2001, 200–29.
——— 'Alain Badiou's Theory of the Subject: The Recommencement of Dialectical Materialism? (Part II)' in *Pli*, Vol. 13, 2002, 173–208.
Brassier, R., 'Presentation as Anti–phenomenon in Alain Badiou's *Being and Event*', *Continental Philosophy Review*, Vol. 39, 2006, 59–77.
Brassier, R. and Toscano, A., 'Postface: Aleatory Rationalism', in *Theoretical Writings*, 2nd edn (London: Continuum, 2004).
Davidson, D., *Essays on Actions and Events* (Oxford: Clarendon Press, 1980).
Formis, B., 'Esthétique des gestes ordinaires dans l'art contemporain', supervisor Prof. Anne Moeglin-Decroix, Department of Philosophy, Sorbonne University Paris I, October 2007, unpublished.
Frege, G., *The Foundations of Arithmetic*, 2nd rev. edn, trans. J. L. Austin, (Evanston, IL: Northwestern University Press, 1980).
Fry, T., *Remakings: Ecology, Design, Philosophy* (Sydney: Envirobook, 1994).
Hallward, P., 'Generic Sovereignty: The Philosophy of Alain Badiou', *Angelaki*, Vol. 3, No., 1998, 87–110.
Hegel, G.W.F., *The Science of Logic*, trans. A.V. Miller (New York: Humanity Books, 1969).
Heidegger, M., *Being and Time*, trans. J. Macquarrie and E. Robinson (Oxford: Blackwell, 1962).
——— *The End of Philosophy*, trans. J. Stambaugh (Chicago: University of Chicago Press, 2003).
Kacem, M. B., *Événement et répétition* (Paris: Tristram, 2004).
——— *Manifeste antiscolastique: l'esprit du nihilisme 2* (Paris: Nous, 2007).
J. Lacan, *Seminar 11: The Four Fundamental Concepts of Psychoanalysis*, trans. A. Sheridan (London: Penguin, 1994).
——— *Seminar I: Freud's Papers on Technique*, trans. John Forrester (Cambridge: Cambridge University Press, 1988).
——— *Écrits*, trans. B. Fink (New York: W. W. Norton, 2007).
Leibniz, G. W., *Philosophical Writings*, trans. J. M. Morris (London: Dent & Sons, 1934).

Lenin, V. I., 'Our revolution', in *Lenin's Collected Works* Volume 33, 2nd English Edition (Moscow: Progress Publishers, 1965).

Miller, J. A., *Un début dans la vie* (Paris: Le cabinet des lettres, 2002).

Nietzsche, F., *The Will to Power*, trans. W. Kaufman and R. J. Hollingdale (New York: Vintage Books, 1968).

—— *Genealogy of Morals*, trans. W. Kaufman and R. J. Hollingdale (New York: Vintage Books, 1989).

Schurmann, R., *Heidegger on Being and Acting* (Indiana: Indiana University Press, 1990).

Toscano, A., 'Marxism Expatriated: Alain Badiou's Turn' in Jacques Bidet and Kouvelakis, S. (eds), *Critical Companion to Contemporary Marxism* (Leiden: E. J. Brill, 2007), 529–48.

Virgil, *The Aeneid*, trans. R. Fagles (New York: Viking Books, 2006).

Žižek, S., *The Ticklish Subject* (London: Verso, 1999).

Name Index

Althusser 1–18, 20–1, 24, 26, 28–9,
    32–3, 36–7, 39, 41, 46, 53, 58,
    67, 73, 96, 109, 111, 119, 121,
    127, 140n.1, 141n.7, 141n.14,
    141n.16, 142n.21, 142n.23,
    142n.24, 144n.48, 144n.50,
    144n.52, 145n.58, 149n.12, 153,
    155–6
Aristotle 6, 9–11, 79, 98, 101, 115,
    119–20, 123, 141n.18,
    149n.17

Bachelard 2, 13, 17, 20–1, 24
Balibar 1, 13–14, 21, 140n.1,
    142n.24, 144n.48, 156
Brassier 101, 148n.7, 149n.18,
    151n.42, 154, 156

Cantor 70, 72, 112, 144n.55
Carnap 1, 3, 22, 23, 144n.53
Celan 116
Cohen 70–1, 110, 112, 125

Davidson 93, 149n.10, 156
Deleuze 33, 40, 48, 105, 142n.19,
    146n.8, 150n.34, 154
Derrida 20, 91, 143n.44,
    151n.46

Foucault 2, 20, 46, 142n.24, 151n.45
Frege 2, 14–18, 22, 24, 92, 142n.29,
    143n.32, 143n.35, 144n.53, 156

Gödel 22, 25–6, 70–1, 143n.44,
    144n.53

Hallward 92, 141n.5, 142n.28,
    145n.3, 149n.24, 152, 153, 155,
    156
Hegel 5–6, 9, 27, 39, 40–4, 48, 50–1,
    56, 73, 78, 87–8, 116, 129,
    146n.4, 156
Heidegger 44, 87–9, 91, 109,
    142n.20, 148n.6, 149n.15, 156

Kant 50, 74, 83, 122, 144n.49

Lacan 3, 15–16, 19, 27–8, 40, 44,
    46–7, 50–2, 54, 57, 61–7, 69, 82,
    89, 101, 113, 115, 124, 129, 132,
    144n.56, 146n.9, 146n.10,
    146n.14, 147n.18, 147n.19,
    147n.20, 151n.46, 156
Lacoue-Labarthe 84, 87, 91, 127,
    148n.1, 148n.4
Lenin 5–7, 35–6, 43, 48, 50, 58, 73,
    77, 95, 104, 141n.9, 145n.59,
    156

Mao 7, 35–6, 50, 54, 58, 73, 78, 85,
    129
Mallarmé 20, 40, 44–6, 100, 102,
    129–32, 151n.46
Marx 4–8, 12–13, 39, 48, 50, 57, 74,
    91, 96

Meyerhold 114
Miller 2, 12, 14–18, 47, 142n.28,
    143n.35, 143n.44, 146n.10, 156

Nancy 84, 87, 117, 127, 148n.1,
    148n.4,
Nietzsche 20, 46, 89, 98, 112, 115–16,
    120–1, 124, 149n.16, 150n.32,
    150n.36, 157

Plato 36, 139

Quine 3, 22, 144n.53

Russell 17, 22, 92, 101, 142n.29,
    144n.53

Sartre 2, 10, 71, 121, 153.